Praise for *Creative Learners*

"Learning is all about relationships, and the inspiring stories in Selma Ridgway's book illustrate that perfectly. All students—especially those who learn differently—need special people in their lives who let them know that they are capable of success and support them along their unique paths. These powerful stories will encourage and inspire struggling students, as well as those who work with them, as they seek their own creative ways to learn and achieve."

—Doro Bush Koch
Honorary Chair, Barbara Bush Foundation for Family Literacy

"Growing up in the segregated south with dyslexia and attention deficit disorder, my escape was facilitated by compassionate and thoughtful teachers like Selma Ridgway, who recognized that different is not a disability, but rather simply a challenge.

Creative Learners offers a comprehensive roadmap for teachers who often struggle with overcrowded classrooms, inadequate facilities, and students who may be unaware of their learning differences. This invaluable resource, told through the prism of students, parents, and teachers, can remarkably reshape the educational paradigm, inspiring many who have been abandoned because they did not fit into a system. Imagine a world where educators utilize differences to motivate students to achieve—Selma Ridgway has opened a portal to that world and we should embrace it forcefully.

As Ambassador to the United Nations, I traveled the world and preached the Gospel of education as the most potent antidote to poverty, racism, and conflict. This marvelous book will be an effective tool for uplifting our 'different children.'"

—Ambassador Andrew Young

"While reading *Creative Learners*, my first thought was how do we get a Selma Ridgway in every public school so we can show every student with a 'learning difference' ways to thrive and to love school? My 13,000 colleagues running America's school systems will feel just like I did when they read these inspiring, real-life stores from students, parents, and teachers. Getting *Creative Learners* into the hands of as many educators as possible must be the first step."

—Daniel A. Domenech
Executive Director, American Association of School Administrators

"Selma Ridgway's important book offers a lifeline to kids struggling with learning differences and highlights the power of the human spirit to triumph over adversity. It informs, educates, inspires, and reminds us that every human being can achieve success in his or her own way."

—Thomas J. Donohue
President and Chief Executive Officer, U.S. Chamber of Commerce

"As an ADD child going through school before the diagnosis was well know, I struggled mightily. I was in the lower third of my class, was constantly in trouble, and I easily might have not made it to adulthood. Instead, I discovered a passion for innovation and challenging the status quo and became an entrepreneur. When reading *Creative Learners*, I couldn't help thinking how easy it could have been for me to not make it at all. If I had access to stories such as those Selma has collected here, I wouldn't have fought my battles alone. If you know someone who is struggling to learn creatively, read this book … better yet, get them a copy."

—Pete Kight
Founder, CheckFree Corporation

"A good teacher leaves a student with a new insight, perspective, or understanding. A great teacher has enough humility and sincerity that they receive the same from their student in return. Selma Ridgway is that great teacher. In *Creative Learner*, Selma reminds us all of the infinite gifts that come from believing in the potential of every child. Great minds do not think alike; they think differently. In *Creative Learners*, Selma puts us all in great company!"

—Josh J. Clark
Head of School, The Schenck School

"*Creative Learners* is a remarkable and inspiring collection of success stories. It was a joy and a delight to read about the incredible and creative people who overcame their so-called 'disabilities' and rose from the abyss of failure to success. The book points out what can be done through creativity and tenacity. However, it is also a painful reminder that we still suffer mightily from a systemic failure of effective ways to rescue people who need help, particularly in learning to read and write. We are still losing too many young people to gang membership, drugs, and crime. It is in the public arena that we are not recognizing the individual differences in our children to save many of them from failure. Where are the public examples of the Woodward Academy's Transition Program and others? If we have them, we need to take another look at their programs. It behooves us to remember the old adage that an ounce of prevention is worth a pound of cure. It is time to renew our efforts to find new ways to teach our young people what they need to know to find the success they deserve."

—**Conley Ingram**
Senior Judge, Cobb Superior Court
Former Cobb Juvenile Court Judge,
Superior Court Judge and Justice,
Supreme Court of Georgia

"The many testimonials recorded in *Creative Learners* prove that we are not defined by our abilities—or lack thereof—but rather our passion, perseverance, and compassion. These elements enable us to overcome obstacles and challenges. These unsung heroes, the loving parents and caring educators who devote untold hours and efforts, see beyond the impossible to help the next generation achieve their dreams.

These creative learners demonstrate hope when all seems hopeless, discovering their talents and unlocking their full potential despite the seemingly crippling obstacles and learning differences. Stars always shine brightest in the darkest of nights. When there is a will, there is a way."

—**Jean Sung**
Head of The Philanthropy Centre, Asia
Hong Kong

"The LD and ADHD community celebrates the uniqueness, practicality, and sagacity of *Creative Learners*. Selma Ridgway assisted high school students in identifying their keys to academic and life success for more than thirty-five years. She now shares her insights in this illuminating book geared for creative learners, educators, and parents alike. Selma's mix of information and inspiration is sure to enlighten and encourage."

—**Jonathan Jones**
Learning Disabilities of America

"If you or a loved one has a learning difference, you must read this book! Its first-person accounts of how young people learned to overcome their learning challenges and succeed will inspire you. This book is a beautiful and moving read. It demonstrates that when young people learn skills to overcome their learning differences, they gain self-confidence, maturity, wisdom, and achieve great success."

—**Susan Stockdale**
Children's Book Author and Illustrator

"The lessons in these stories speak to the resilience, ability, and determination creative learners demonstrate on a daily basis. Not only will you be inspired by these messages, you will gain insight on how to support students and young adults struggling to find their way and make their mark on the world. You will find answers, suggestions, and great strategies that will enrich your journey with this dynamic population."

—**John Wilson**
Executive Director, SOAR

"Inspiring! Whether you are a student struggling with learning differences or a parent or teach working with those individuals, Creative Learners is a must read. These first-hand accounts delve honestly into the personal challenges for anyone dealing with learning difficulties, while offering much-needed hope for the future."

—**Rebecca Ruffin Leffler,**
Freelance Writer and Parent of a Learning-Challenged Teen

CREATIVE LEARNERS

CREATIVE LEARNERS

STORIES OF INSPIRATION AND SUCCESS
from People with Dyslexia, ADD, or Other Learning Differences

SELMA RIDGWAY

Published by Advantage, Charleston, South Carolina.
Member of Advantage Media Group.

ADVANTAGE is a registered trademark, and the Advantage colophon is a trademark of Advantage Media Group, Inc.

Printed in the United States of America.

10 9 8 7 6 5 4 3 2 1

ISBN: 978-1-64225-016-9
LCCN: 2018932627

Cover design by Melanie Cloth.
Layout design by George Stevens.

This publication is designed to provide accurate and authoritative information in regard to the subject matter covered. It is sold with the understanding that the publisher is not engaged in rendering legal, accounting, or other professional services. If legal advice or other expert assistance is required, the services of a competent professional person should be sought.

Advantage Media Group is proud to be a part of the Tree Neutral® program. Tree Neutral offsets the number of trees consumed in the production and printing of this book by taking proactive steps such as planting trees in direct proportion to the number of trees used to print books. To learn more about Tree Neutral, please visit **www.treeneutral.com**.

Advantage Media Group is a publisher of business, self-improvement, and professional development books and online learning. We help entrepreneurs, business leaders, and professionals share their Stories, Passion, and Knowledge to help others Learn & Grow. Do you have a manuscript or book idea that you would like us to consider for publishing? Please visit **advantagefamily.com** or call **1.866.775.1696**.

To all creative learners.

FOREWORD

Selma Ridgway has given us inspiring stories about remarkable people who have overcome tremendous obstacles through courage, resourcefulness, perseverance, and grit. I love that it is called *Creative Learners* because students who learn differently must be very creative indeed in order to succeed in mainstream environments that do not always recognize their gifts. I know this from personal experience.

Back when I was in public school, learning differences were not as well understood as they are today, and we didn't have the tools and strategies to develop the skills needed to accommodate our differences. As a result, I always thought I was dumb, and my teachers did too. At one point, my mother was called in and told to take me out of school because I couldn't handle the work. I always felt inferior, ashamed and embarrassed, and those feelings would remain with me well into adulthood.

I had trouble with reading, or rather, with remembering and processing what I'd just read. I could read the words but they didn't imprint on my brain—it might as well have been a blank page. It wasn't until many years later that I actually found out that this was a recognized condition. When my daughter was having trouble learning, we brought her for an assessment at The Lab School in Washington, DC. She was reluctant to take the test so, to ease her anxiety, I offered to take it with her. When the Director came back with the results, she looked at me and said "obviously, you also learn differently." I broke down in tears ... at last, there was an explanation for the pain I'd been experiencing my entire life.

Like a lot of kids who learn differently, I got into trouble ... a lot. The bitter frustration and deep humiliation that I always felt in class would bubble over into anger, and I would act up both in school and out. I ran around with a tough crowd, some of whom would later end up in prison, or dead. I was lucky to have been given a second chance by the intervention of a caring mentor who believed in me and gave me hope that I had a future.

It is estimated that learning differences may affect as many as 15% to 20% of the population. On one hand, it's interesting to note that an inordinate number of highly successful individuals are people with learning differences ... and some of them are commonly called geniuses. Albert Einstein, Thomas Edison, Steve Jobs, Steven Spielberg, Charles Schwab, Magic

Johnson, baseball great Nolan Ryan, Richard Branson, Whoopi Goldberg, Andrew Young, the late Payne Stewart, and so many others in every field of endeavor have overcome learning challenges to achieve the highest levels of success. Creative learners, indeed. But others are not always so fortunate, and we also know that today, with an estimated 10 million students who learn differently in our schools throughout the US, we have many at risk of being underserved, of becoming dropouts, and/or inmates and never realizing the joy of their creative minds.

Because of my own learning difficulties, I've always felt a special empathy for those who struggle to succeed in school and, when I finally got my own act together, I made a lifelong commitment to help underserved young people complete their education. In some ways, the Communities In Schools movement began more than 40 years ago as a direct result of the pain I experienced personally as well as the challenges that I witnessed in so many other young people. Fortunately, there are now many other organizations and institutions that not only recognize but also celebrate and cultivate the inherent potential of different learners.

Furthermore, there is a wealth of resources available to empower teachers, counselors, medical staff, parents, and students themselves to discover their gifts and develop the skills necessary to achieve their dreams. This book – with its stories of resilience and determination, hope and triumph – is a tremendous addition to that arsenal. The stories told here, voiced by individuals who have overcome potentially crippling obstacles, are testaments to the fortitude of the human spirit and the resolve to succeed despite the odds. Selma Ridgway has created a unique and powerful chronicle of these journeys, which affirm the fundamental principle that, with appropriate supports, all students can learn.

Creative Learners will inspire parents, teachers, scientists and other leaders to seek new ways to unlock potential and overcome pain. Then many millions still trapped will discover their gifts, will themselves become creative learners, achieve and give back.

Bill Milliken

Founder of Communities In Schools

Noted Author

Advisor to three US Presidents

Recipient of the National Jefferson Award for Public Service

ACKNOWLEDGMENTS

To all creative learners: We honor and thank you for sharing your unique gifts. I give special thanks to those who have allowed me to be a part of their journey and have enriched my life with their incredible successes. To all who have shared your stories in this book: many thanks. We are also indebted to the teachers and parents of creative learners who were gracious in sharing their stories of inspiration and success. In addition, I thank Jane King, long time teacher of English to creative learners, for helping to collect and edit some of the stories in this book.

Many thanks to the Lanigan Insurance Group (LIG) who provided inspiration and funding for the book and who, in 2004, established the endowment at Woodward Academy to fund the annual Transition College Scholarship Award to a deserving Woodward graduate. Several of the contributors to this book were recipients of the award.

Special thanks to The Dyslexia Resource of the Schenck School for embracing the Creative Learners Project and to Bill

Milliken and Neil Shorthouse for supporting the project and allowing it to be a part of the Communities in Schools organization to help teachers across America diagnosis and address learning differences.

Special thanks to the staff at Advantage publishing for their patience, support, encouragement, and guidance throughout the collection and preparation of these stories.

TABLE OF CONTENTS

SHARING THE VOICES OF CREATIVE LEARNERS

I n the early 1980s, when I was a counselor and a teacher of mathematics at Woodward Academy, I agreed to direct what is now known as the Transition Program. Woodward was one of the first schools in metro Atlanta to establish a program to educate students with diagnosed learning differences in a college preparatory setting. The program was on the cutting edge, and as its new and rather inexperienced director (I'm not sure I could have defined dyslexia at the time), I had an enormous amount to learn. One of the first and most important lessons was that students with diagnosed learning disabilities are capable of being as successful as any of their nondisabled peers, but they expend extraordinary effort to reach the same level of achievement. Nonconventional learners have to master the same difficult college-prep curriculum as their classmates, but as one student wrote, they also have to "learn how to learn it." My learning curve was steep, but the students taught me, and I remain indebted to them. At

1

graduation time, as these courageous students who persevered through rigorous academic challenges crossed the stage—many with substantial scholarships—I longed to shout words of congratulations for the world to hear. I knew how much had gone into their special moment: the long hours of study, the occasional frustrations, the many tested strategies, and the creative

> *One of the first and most important lessons was that students with diagnosed learning disabilities are capable of being as successful as any of their nondisabled peers, but they expend extraordinary effort to reach the same level of achievement.*

approaches to learning.

Later, when parents reported success in college and beyond, I once again longed to shout praises from the rooftops. When a friend with experience in learning differences offered to fund this book project, I knew that the dream of a lifetime would come true. I never wanted to "write" a book in my words, but I longed to share the voices of the individuals who had achieved so much. The amazing stories in this book are representative of hundreds of others who have managed learning differences through patience, courage, creativity, and perseverance. They have endured tough environments and met difficult demands to make their dreams come true, educating and inspiring teachers, peers, parents, and administrators like myself along the way. They conquered the demands of the world with the flow of their creative minds, unique visions, and personal passions.

Many of those who contributed essays to this book attended Woodward Academy. Some attended the Schenck School, or the Atlanta Speech School. These three institutions are at the hub of innovative approaches to learning differences in Atlanta, and their strategies are applicable to all students who learn differently.

One purpose of this book is to honor different learners who have inspiring stories to tell, and another is to provide examples for those still struggling to find success.

The 2017 report from the National Center for Learning Disabilities stated, " Children with learning and attention issues number one in five in the general population, and though they are as smart as their peers and can achieve at high levels, too often they are misunderstood as lazy or unintelligent. Without the right academic support, they are more likely than their peers to repeat a grade, get suspended, and dropout. These struggling individuals have trouble in the work place and have high rates of involvement with the criminal justice system. one-third of incarcerated youth have a specific learning disability, and one half of those released return to confinement in 3 years." The individuals whose stories are told in this book were lucky to receive proper help in time to learn to maximize their strengths and manage their non-strengths. For those who have not been lucky enough to receive needed help, it is our hope that these stories will inspire them to reach out to the Dyslexia Resource, the International Dyslexia Association, the Learning Disabilities Association, or another organization which provides assistance to creative learners.

Our contributors come from all walks of life: student, lawyer, banker, actor, artist, engineer, Navy SEAL, businessperson. Despite that diversity, common themes emerge from their stories. Many write that they experienced breakthroughs when they realized that they could complete a task or absorb information if they devoted extra time to it ("Show up early and stay late," as one said). Developing self-knowledge was the key to success in a wide variety of endeavors, from college studies to business advancement, and the strategy of using strengths to manage nonstrengths also played a pivotal role. One of the most common epiphanies for those who learn differently was the realization that discovering and following a personal passion made everything easier. Perhaps the most inspiring advice from our contributors is *find your passion and follow it.* Like so much of the wisdom in these pages, it is good advice for all of us, whatever our individual learning styles.

> *One of the most common epiphanies for those who learn differently was the realization that discovering and following a personal passion made everything easier.*

The exemplary ability of the authors of these stories to overcome roadblocks often resulted in heightened compassion and a desire to help those labeled as "different." One of the big takeaways from this book, and my decades in education, is that we all learn differently. Accepting that we all have different learning styles makes stigmatizing students who need a little extra time on tests or assistive technology for reading seem ridiculous. The success of contributors who went on to become partners in big law firms, to star in major theater productions, and to start thriving businesses should put to rest any notion that a particular learning style is a reflection of talent or intelligence.

> *Accepting that we all have different learning styles makes stigmatizing students who need a little extra time on tests or assistive technology for reading seem ridiculous.*

Some learning differences are deep enough that they require more creative approaches. With that in mind, I have included a chapter of stories written by parents and another one by teachers. These pieces reflect both groups' willingness to be flexible, to change plans, to listen, to accommodate, and improvise to support the unique learner in finding successful strategies. Accommodations and creative approaches in the classroom often benefit all learners. In the words of one great educator, what works for the student with a learning disability will probably be good for all students.

The creative learner who struggles with conventional guidance might well be the most successful individual in the class. With this in mind, these stories validate action by educators to embrace different learners in all schools. These stories of inspiration and success from people with dyslexia, attention deficit disorder (ADD), or other learning differences reflect the use of creative, and resourceful talents and are intended to honor the authors and inspire others along the way.

CHAPTER 1

MY JOURNEY

When Henley Kibler came to Woodward Academy, two things stood out: his dyslexia was severe, and he was one of the most gifted individuals I have ever known. He struggled with language in school and spent untold hours completing his homework, but he still had time to be very active in extracurricular activities. One year, when the Fourth of July fell on a Sunday, Henley ran in Atlanta's famous Peachtree Road Race. Later that morning, he gave the children's sermon at church, sharing with the congregation what it felt like to complete the 10K.

Having worked in the production end of theater for several years, Henley decided to try acting and earned the part of Edna Turnblad in productions of *Hairspray* at both school and church. He became the Woodard Academy mascot, working with the cheerleaders in his War Eagle costume, and when he went to Belmont University in Nashville, he became a cheerleader there, even though he spent long hours on his schoolwork. He followed his passion for sound production into a career he loves. Henley's unique journey is notable for the many ways he learned to advocate for himself and to maximize his gifts in order to validate who he is.

My name is Henley Kibler and my learning disabilities have never stopped me from reaching my goals. I have come a very long way and overcome a lot of obstacles that seemed impossible. I was able to meet challenges that seemed overwhelming at the time because of three important things. First is the support of my family; second, my utilization of technology; and third, amazing teachers who were a whole lot more patient than I was.

My Favorite thing to do is to swim.   9/h/18

When I was six, the drawing pictured here was among my finest work. This was done about a year after I was diagnosed with dyslexia, dysgraphia, and ADHD. At this time, I had just transferred from my local public school to the

Atlanta Speech School, which focused on helping kids with learning disabilities. In my young mind, I didn't really see a problem with a "special" school. In fact, I liked it more. They had longer recess, and that is all a six-year-old could really ask for.

The Atlanta Speech School helped form a foundation that allowed me to adapt to a world that does not accommodate people with dyslexia and dysgraphia. The classrooms utilized smart screens and lots of technology, a new approach to learning at that time. The new school also had a different class structure that focused on reading. Most important, they taught me how to advocate for myself. This strategy was invaluable and helped me acquire important life skills. I learned to ask for help and figured out new ways of doing old things.

I went to this school from first grade to sixth grade. As I grew up, I also had an amazing support system at home, which is the fundamental reason I was able to accommodate my disabilities. Reading was very hard and took an enormous amount of time, but my parents did everything they could to help. Every night they would sit with me for hours, helping me read stories, and answering my questions about them.

My dad found screen-reading software that allowed you to scan in the text, so that the computer could read it back to you. The program would read text to me, highlighting words so that I could read along with it. Screen-reading technology was very new then, was not always accurate, and used some very weird voices. But it really sped up the process and helped improve my reading. This software also allowed me to fill in the blanks by typing instead of having to write words down, a game changer for me. At this time, all of the homework I got was in a workbook, so every page had to be scanned in for the screen reader to read it. When I finished an assignment, I had to print all the answers. Despite the difficulties, this method was still easier than reading and writing on my own.

I learned hundreds of tricks to more easily do things that had seemed impossible: spelling tricks, test-taking tricks, counting tricks, reading tricks … the list goes on. Without these tricks, I wouldn't have been able to function in school or in everyday society. I also learned what I am good at and what I am bad at, what distracts me and what helps me focus. But the most important thing I took away from that school was the belief that *nothing is impossible.*

> *The most important thing I took away from that school was the belief that nothing is impossible.*

As I started to think about leaving this school and moving to middle school, my parents dropped a bombshell that made me feel dumber than I ever had in my life. They told me that I was going to repeat the sixth grade. I thought school was already hard enough, so why would I want to do more? When I asked why I would have to repeat, they said it would make the transition to middle school easier. To me, though, repeating meant that I was dumb and had messed up. For months, I would get home from school and try to convince my parents that I didn't need to repeat. They would hold their ground, and I would go to sleep crying. Every time we argued, I said, "I will try harder and do better. Please don't make me do this! School is so hard, and you are making me do the same grade over again." I would be leaving all of my friends by staying in the sixth grade, and for the rest of my education, I would have to explain why I was older than my peers.

When I look back now, though, I am glad my parents stuck to their guns. Their decision probably kept me from hating school forever. If I hadn't repeated sixth grade, I would have failed the seventh grade and, ultimately, might have dropped out of school. Staying in that school another year allowed me to take advantage of its great disabilities department, which further pushed me to use technology to accommodate my disabilities. Many of the classes included kids just like me, with learning disabilities. The thing I worried about most—and still do—was reading something out loud. I feared being called on to read in class or, worst of all, to write on the board. These are things that I have struggled with my entire life, and they are still huge fears. I still feel embarrassment when people struggle to read my handwriting or say, "That isn't even close to how you spell that" or "Never mind. I will just read it." These aren't things you ever really overcome, but you can be prepared for them, which helps the situation.

I made it through that second year of sixth grade and moved on to middle school, where there were no classes strictly for learning-disabled kids. All students were mixed together. I was so nervous! Because of my dysgraphia, I had learned to type my notes on the computer, which many of the kids in this class would have never seen before. I was allowed to do that even though the other students weren't. Likewise, I was allowed additional time because of my slow reading rate. I was afraid other kids would ask why I could take more time on tests than they did. These fears never went away, and the questions were asked regularly. I learned to answer them and try to explain my disability to educate my fellow students, and I found that was the best solution.

Something I wasn't prepared for, though, was the increased reading workload. I had gotten pretty good at scanning my assignments into the computer every night. That had taken me an extra ten to fifteen minutes to do when I had ten pages or so. But in middle school, the reading really picked up. Soon it was thirty to forty pages a night. Another difficulty was that we started to use hardcover textbooks, so to properly scan a page, you had to cut it out of the book. Otherwise, it wouldn't fit flat in the scanner. This really took some time. Fortunately, for most books, textbook manufacturers started making digital copies available along with hard copies.

Luckily, my dad stepped in to help me with this, but it took a lot of time to cut pages out of a 700-page textbook and scan them, and at the end of that process, the textbook was worthless, its pages loose, crinkled, and out of order. My dad helped a lot, but the man-hours I put in were still about double or triple those of my class-mates. Over time, I learned that this was okay. That was just how it had to be for me to learn. In high school, the workload increased even more, and grades really started to matter. I faced many of the same challenges once again, and again, I had great help. A tutor worked with me early on Saturday mornings, and great teachers played to my strengths.

I had to spend more hours on schoolwork than many students in order to succeed, but I still found time for extracurricular activities, especially communications. I was first introduced to the technical side of this field at First Presbyterian Church of Atlanta, where I worked in the broadcast ministry during my middle school years. I learned all about broadcasting and the running of the service, from operating cameras to handling live and recorded audio. I stayed very involved with this through middle school and high school, learning various jobs and moving up to be an assistant broadcast director. I also was in charge of all the youth musical audio. In high school, I became part of the AV department and really enjoyed the behind-the-scenes aspects of it all. I enjoyed thinking the logistics out and being able to figure out technical solutions for any problems.

Participating in extracurricular activities in high school and graduating with decent grades helped get me into the college I wanted to attend. High school was a difficult adjustment, but college was a whole different game. The reading was crazy! The first semester was really hard for me. I recently found this note that I wrote to myself at that time:

My dyslexia is truly affecting me this year. My inability to pickup concepts as fast as a traditional learner is making it very hard. I work my hardest and spend a lot of time on every subject and give everything my best, but the work load doesn't let me do as good as I feel I could. I am using all my accommodations in classes and all my resources outside of class but still can't keep up. I want to be great! I work all night and finally finish with poor work because my brain is so tired. I feel truly disabled, almost stupid. I feel as though college isn't for me. I want to learn everything, but there is not time for that. There isn't even time for me to be average. But I can do my best always and never let anyone tell me I didn't try or that I am stupid. I can do anything that I want to do. It might take longer but I can do it. I have made it this far in my life. I must remain strong and motivated and never give up. Giving up is admitting I can't do something. And I can do anything I try, but unlike others I have overcome adversity that they will never encounter, and that adversity has made me strong beyond measure. I am unstoppable. Many say that I didn't try. Contrary to their belief I tried very hard. The world was not made for me. If anything, it was made to destroy me and brake me down. But I will make it to the top of the mountain. The success will be short lived because as soon as I get to the top I will see that there is an even taller mountain to climb. I will power through the pain of climbing this mountain and make it to the top, and like before, there will be an even taller mountain awaiting. But what am I gonna do? Give up? No, I will defeat the opponent of life. I will never give up. Nothing will make me stop. Every mountain is a different challenge that I must concur.[1]

College is where the need to advocate for myself became important. I got close to the disabilities coordinator, and she helped me with books and my individual education plan. I met with all my professors early in the semester and reviewed accommodations with them. I found that most of the professors really wanted to help me and were cooperative. Only once did I have a professor who refused to let me use my computer in class. And I found that, sometimes, a C+ can become a B- if you bake the teacher a triple chocolate cake.

---

[1]   Author's note: misspellings and grammar have not been edited.

In May 2016 I graduated from Belmont University with a BS degree in audio engineering. It was a very special day for my family and me. I even made the dean's list during the last two semesters. Early college included a lot of reading and writing. As I moved up, though, the work was more practical and logical for my major. I did well in those classes and found work in my field when I graduated.

I fell in love with live production work from the beginning. I felt passionate about it because it was an area in which I could excel and something many of my peers couldn't do. I still love the constant problem solving that is required for live services, concerts, sports, and other events. Audio is constantly changing and never boring. Studying it gave me confidence, goals, and direction.

Being able to work in an area of strength makes me feel smart and useful. It is also great to make money doing something you love. As I write this, I'm excited that I'm about to go on tour with the 2016 winner of the Country Music Association's Album of the Year award, Eric Church.

I feel lucky that my disabilities have taught me so much about myself. Many of my friends and colleagues haven't had to really think about their strengths and weaknesses or to overcome embarrassment and adversity.

I feel lucky that my disabilities have taught me so much about myself. Many of my friends and colleagues haven't had to really think about their strengths and weaknesses or to overcome embarrassment and adversity. I have learned a lot about life and about myself. I have learned that the world is not made for my learning style. I have learned that I have to work harder and longer than most to accomplish certain tasks. I have learned that there will be times when certain things seem impossible to overcome. But nothing is impossible and, without my disability, I wouldn't be who I am today.

—Henley Kibler

CHAPTER 2

DRIVEN BY THE DIFFERENCE

"He probably will never learn to read and write." That was the grim prediction given to Drake's parents as he began his journey through school. The class snickered when Chelsea proudly announced that the second day of the week was "Tonday." Glenn did not understand why math and science had to be so hard when English and history were easy. Drake, Chelsea, and Glenn had to face the realities of the impact of their diagnosed learning disabilities.

As did their classmates, they had to master the designated curriculum for each grade level. But before they could master academic content, they had to develop their own unique ways of learning various subjects. These three, as did others whose stories appear in this book, quickly discovered that they could not rely on incidental learning, not even at an early age. If they were to learn, the approach had to be intentional.

Through long hours of hard work and guidance by caring families and teachers, our contributors in Chapter 2 developed an understanding of their learning differences, accepted that they had to work differently from their peers, and dedicated themselves to finding strategies for success. Through intentional planning, they adopted routines that worked for their unique learning styles: organizing materials impeccably, finding a quiet place to work and test, using flash cards or note cards, optimizing the visual over the auditory or vice versa.

The techniques discovered by these individuals helped develop the skills that led to success, and they also led to a heightened awareness of others' struggles and a desire to share and give back. Chelsea is obtaining a master's degree in mental health counseling. Drake, happily married with two children and a managerial position with Chick-fil-A, gives back in his community and church every day. Glenn has come full-circle and is now employed by the school where he himself once struggled with math and science. The director of development at Woodward had this to say about Glenn, "Glenn is the strongest major gift officer with whom I have worked in my thirty years in the profession."

DRIVEN BY THE DIFFERENCE

In elementary school, I struggled to comprehend information quickly and was diagnosed with a learning disability. In the fourth and fifth grades, I was fortunate enough to attend a school for children with learning disabilities where I learned strategies that helped me cope with my learning differences. I realized that I was a visual learner. I also learned to become my own advocate, asking for help whenever I needed it.

PREKINDERGARTEN

"Chelsea, what's the second day of the week?" my teacher asked.

T ... didn't a day begin with that letter? Oh, I'm not sure! I struggled to remember the name of the correct day as my classmates raised their hands eagerly and cried, "I know! I know!" They knew. Why didn't I?

"Okay, Chelsea, what will it be?"

My cheeks burned as I blurted an answer I hoped was right: "Tonday." Immediately the room exploded with noise. *Had I been right?* No. That sound was laughter, and it was directed at me.

THIRD GRADE

"Sweetie, are you okay?" asked Dad when he'd finished talking. *I must act brave.* Eyebrows furrowed, I shrugged and looked the other way. He had just explained to me that I had a learning disability and needed to transfer to the Atlanta Speech School, a place for kids with learning differences. Dad wrapped his arms around my hunched shoulders as I finally burst into tears. I could only imagine my new school filled with creepy, strange, and stupid kids.

FOURTH GRADE

"There you go. You've got it!" my Atlanta Speech School teacher said, applauding when I finished acting out the meaning of the verb *to cringe*. I got it? I got it right! Who would have thought that acting out definitions of words would ease my difficulties with processing information quickly and comprehending main ideas? Encouraged, I determined to accumu-late more coping strategies. By the end of fifth grade,

I was ready to apply to a "normal" school. How would I handle this change?

SEVENTH GRADE

"Just write it down and ask about it later," said my English teacher. The advice might sound simple, but it had a profound impact on my life. It relieved me of the pressure and urgency I felt to comprehend information as soon as it was presented. Knowing that I could make sense of it later helped me make it through classes without letting my frustration sabotage the learning process.

TENTH GRADE

No one spoke a word. They just stared at me. Was that a good sign? I had just volunteered my first analytical connection in English class after spending half of my first year barely speaking at Georgetown Day School. My teacher finally broke the silence: "Chelsea, that's a remarkable connection you just made." My peers slowly came to life and nodded in agreement. I beamed. Perhaps I had underestimated my ability to comprehend "big pictures." It was the first time at this new school that I did not feel as if I were trying to run through snow.

ELEVENTH GRADE

"Ask Chelsea. She can explain it," remarked a student in my math class to a confused friend. It was hard for me to believe that students were beginning to flock to *me* when they were bewildered, complimenting me on my patience and predicting a teaching career in my future. It was true that I relished the rewarding moment when someone smiled with understanding after my explanations. My teaching passion drew me to a summer internship at the Lab School of Washington, where I worked with children who had learning disabilities. I could sympathize with their experiences. I understood that "I can't" really meant "This is hard," and I knew to interpret "I won't" as "I'm afraid."

I understood that "I can't" really meant "This is hard," and I knew to interpret "I won't" as "I'm afraid."

TODAY

Sometimes, I wish I could snap my fingers and make my learning disability disappear. When those times come up, though, I remind myself how fortunate I am to have my health, parents, a brother I love, and friends I enjoy. I realize that I would never have become the focused, determined worker I am now if I had not lived life with my learning difference. Each step I took in this journey of my learning struggle enabled me to take pride in the person that I am today.

I now refer to myself as "a person with a learning disability" rather than as "learning disabled." This highlights the fact that I am a human being first, and a human being with a unique way of learning second. This linguistic distinction reminds me that my learning disability does not define me.

By applying the study strategies and self-knowledge I gained during my two years at the Atlanta Speech School, I managed to thrive academically.

I earned straight As at Woodward Academy, where I attended the Transition Program from sixth to eighth grade and the College Prep Program in ninth grade. I graduated from Georgetown Day School with a GPA of 4.0 and from Hamilton College *summa cum laude* as a member of Phi Beta Kappa. As I write this, I am maintaining a GPA of 4.0 at DePaul University. My journey has taught me the value of patience, perseverance, and advocacy in pursuing personal needs.

As far as I have come academically, though, I have never forgotten where I started. In fact, my experience of overcoming a learning disability inspired me to become a counselor. I want to help others identify coping strategies for developing healthier behavior, which is why I am pursuing a master's degree in clinical mental health counseling at DePaul.

—Chelsea

CLIMBING MOUNTAINS

From the very beginning, school was extremely difficult for me. To say that first grade was a challenge would be an understatement. As my first-grade class was learning to read, it quickly became clear that I was not functioning at the same level as my peers. I wasn't learning to read. As the rest of the class climbed that mountain, I fell off a cliff.

My parents had me tested to understand why I was struggling in school. We all have lasting memories, and for me, the day the psychologist shared those test results will forever top the list. My parents and I were told that I probably would never learn to read or write. As if that weren't hard enough to hear, this diagnosis also gave me no chance of finishing school or going on to college.

The more important memories for me, though, the ones I choose to focus on, are all the ways my parents stood by me. They were determined to help me learn how to learn. I give complete credit to my Lord and Savior for everything I have accomplished in my life, but my mom and dad deserve thanks too. They never gave up on me. They continued to push through all the struggles and pain, even when I couldn't.

I started school at Woodward Academy, and then my parents placed me in a public school in Morrow, Georgia, which had a program to help children with learning diffi-culties. At Morrow, I repeated the first grade and started working with a speech therapist. I had a terrible stutter at the time. I stayed at Morrow through the fifth grade, and then my parents decided to move me back to Woodward Academy.

When I returned to my previous school, I tested well enough to enter the sixth grade. However, after meeting with Mr. Cobb, the principal, my parents made the difficult decision to hold me back and place me in the fifth grade again. That turned out to be the right choice, and so was returning to Woodward. I will forever be grateful to administrators Bill Cobb and Andy Philips for their encouragement and support.

It's hard to explain all the ways Woodward and its teachers helped me, but here are some of the things that helped get me over steep peaks.

For starters, the Transition Program provided students with a lot of security. The classrooms were smaller, and teachers gave students extended time to take tests outside the classroom. The teachers were understanding, and students got to know them well. The daily study period students had with their Transition teacher, was the academic version of a security blanket.

I struggled with planning and organizing my work. Executive processing was one of my biggest challenges, but teachers helped me develop organizing strategies. I learned how to manage my time by using study calendars, planning for each day, week, month, and year. Each calendar had steps to help me develop and follow the process, and I also had a daily check list to make tasks manageable.

Note cards became my other best friend. I made note cards for everything from spelling words to science facts. Using them forced me to write information down, to say it, and to focus on one fact at a time. They also automatically created the repetition that I needed to learn.

In the seventh and eighth grades, I worked with Jane King on study strategies. She helped me to approach information by thinking of it as a story, and in this way, I was able to remember and commit the information to long-term memory. Jane King also helped me learn how to take tests. I was not a strong or fast reader, so test taking scared me. I would get stuck reading a hard question over and over and then, in frustration, rush through the rest of the test. Mrs. King helped me learn how to find and answer the less intimidating questions first. This helped build the confidence I needed to attack the questions I got stuck on.

I also started taking tests by myself, with teacher supervision. In the classroom, seeing other students finish their tests while I continued to struggle was frustrating. I compared myself to them and was discouraged. Taking tests without that distraction allowed me to relax and to focus on the test, not speed.

I continued developing strategies in high school, where Mrs. Stephenson was my study period teacher. It was with Mrs. Stephenson that I learned how to organize research papers by using a note card organizer. She helped me sharpen and practice the skills previously learned in the seventh and eighth grades, adding to the foundation.

The Transition Program helped me become a good student partly by teaching me study skills, but just as important, it provided a place where I could ask the questions I needed to ask, ones I might have been embarrassed to ask in class. I wasn't judged or measured by a test score there. Instead, the focus was on me as an individual and how I could be the best me possible.

All creative learners and their parents need to understand that the struggles these students deal with will never go away—and that's okay. My struggles shaped me into the person I am today. They have given me a greater appreciation for others and the hardships they face.

The academic challenges I faced in high school taught me that life is hard and not fair. The teachers helped me understand and taught me how to work harder than most.

By the time I was a junior at Woodward, I had moved out of the Transition Program and into all college-prep classes. I graduated from the University of Georgia (UGA) in four years, with a degree in consumer economics. For over eighteen years now, I have worked for Chick-fil-A, where I am a manager in Corporate Distribution and Logistics, a subdepartment of our Supply Chain Department.

I climbed steep mountains in pursuit of my educational and career goals, and I'm glad that I had parents and teachers who helped me up every incline instead of believing those early dire predictions that I would never learn to read or finish school.

—Drake

FROM STUDENT TO EMPLOYEE

I came to the Woodward Academy (WA) Transition Program from the Atlanta Speech School in the sixth grade and graduated in 2004. The move was a big change for me. The Atlanta Speech School is very small and caters to children with learning differences. My new school is much bigger, with students of varying abilities. Both in the classroom and out of it, the new curriculum was challenging at the beginning.

The Transition Program helped me in many ways and is the reason I eventually was able to succeed in the classroom. It gave me the opportunity to succeed in small classes with more individualized instruction than other programs offer. In high school, I struggled with numbers, graphs, spreadsheets, and anything related to math or science. The instructors offered extra tutorial sessions to supplement lessons learned in the classroom. I always took advantage of this additional help because I figured out that this was the way I was going to succeed. I gradually learned that if I worked hard and studied as much as I could, I could pass my math and science classes. I was very good at English, history, and other language-based subjects, though word problems in math gave me lots of trouble. I had great difficulty connecting the dots to even understand what the question was asking.

I didn't absorb math or science or anything involving numbers in typical ways, but I discovered strengths that helped me learn in different ways. I used my organizational skills to my advantage in the classroom. I made it a point to have all of my notes well organized so that they were easy to understand while I was studying. I learned to make flash cards for vocabulary words, to use highlighters for note taking, and to find a quiet place with no distractions to get my homework done.

I feel very grateful for all the resources I was offered, most notably extended time on tests. I took advantage of this, as it allowed me to collect my thoughts, think about my answers, and put my best foot forward. I had instructors who really knew how to teach different learners. Their method of teaching students allowed each to come to the material and absorb it in his or her own way.

I am so glad Woodward and the Atlanta Speech School, both Atlanta icons, have kept up good relations over the years. Many kids in Atlanta wouldn't have been able to prosper and succeed without these special schools. Both contributed to my success, and I owe thanks to both places. I was the first recipient of the Selma Ridgway Prize, a cash award for a student who has taken advantage of the services offered by the school. I graduated from Auburn University, where I majored in mass communications. After graduation, I worked for six years, producing a daily sports talk radio show in Atlanta. The organizational skills I learned in high school were essential to my success in directing this program. Next, I worked in fundraising for the nonprofit Children's

Healthcare of Atlanta. I always stayed in touch with WA, and in 2015, I was offered a position there in Advancement, as the principal gifts officer. As I write this, I have been working at WA for fifteen months.

While most schools can only successfully educate students with one type of learning style, the school I attended can successfully educate those who need a rigorous traditional course load and those, like myself, who need the structure and smaller class size that the Transition Program offers. Because of the skills I adopted at WA, I succeeded, academically, which resulted in a growing confidence overall. I grew in my ability to build relationships, and I maintained my positive approach to life.

—Glenn

CHAPTER 3

OUTRUNNING THE ODDS

What do a practicing attorney, a bonds salesman, an administrator for Hilton Worldwide, a financial advisor, and a college sophomore have in common? The five people who share their stories in this chapter all outran the odds to reach a high degree of success. They all found themselves in academic situations that proved difficult beyond expectations because of a learning disability—and succeeded anyway.

"She will never be able to do math or anything else," Rose's fifth-grade teacher pronounced. At another school, a teacher held up Kevin's math paper in class to explain that he had not only done the work incorrectly but also failed to keep up with his peers. For William, writing a paper meant using a large font and wide margins to fill up the page with as few words as possible. Matt received an F- on a paper, and Brooke's parents were advised that college was not in her future.

How did these five individuals overcome negative expectations and obvious academic difficulties to become outstanding professionals? Each found his or her own way. Kevin had to discover a blueprint for his learning style, one he has used throughout his academic and professional life. Rose decided that no one could tell her she would not be successful. Whether it was rope climbing, playing the violin, or taking advanced-level courses, William accepted that he had to work longer and harder than his peers to reach his desired level of success. Matt applied his growth mindset to move beyond the F-, and Brooke ignored those who said something would be too hard for her, whether it was a rigorous college-prep curriculum or cheerleading routines.

Setting goals that at times appeared beyond their grasp, Rose, Kevin, William, Matt, and Brooke found the strategies that allowed them to outrun the odds.

DON'T TELL ME I CAN'T

When everyone else was reading and doing math in school, I had to sit with the teacher. I could not read the simplest book. The teacher suggested an academic evaluation and, based on the test results, I was enrolled in the Schenck School, which works with students who have dyslexia. Finally, I learned to read. My teacher, however, told my parents that I would never be able to do math. At the Schenck School, I began to feel less of a failure because I was not the only one unable to read. All my peers were struggling with the same problems.

> *I devised a mantra—"Brains and strength"—wrote it on the refrigerator door, and went to work.*

At an early age, I applied my strong growth mindset to set goals to stretch myself. When I was invited to a bar mitzvah party where the group was going to be rope climbing, rather than decline, I devised a mantra—"Brains and strength"—wrote it on the refrigerator door, and went to work. By the time I attended the party, no one knew that just a short time earlier I could not climb.

I continued to learn how to persevere when I went to Woodward Academy. More than anything else, I wanted to be in regular classes. I felt that taking special classes was using my learning disability as a crutch, so I pushed myself to become "normal."

My drive to excel extended to music too. At an early age, my parents decided that playing the violin would be good for me. I immediately developed a love-hate relationship with the instrument. I loved the music, but because of my dyslexia, I had great difficulty playing while looking at notes on a page. I couldn't read and play the notes simultaneously. Making an enormous effort to overcome this problem, I practiced until I became one of the better performers in the string group in grade school.

In middle school, it was hard to make myself practice, and yet, playing the violin became an outlet for some of my ADD energy. Also, I liked the sense of belonging that came from being in the orchestra. Rather than give up, I worked even harder. Becoming the best player in the string group became my passion. I played with a group at school and in a community orchestra, and I took private lessons! In the tenth grade, my efforts were rewarded when I was chosen to play with an elite school group called the String Machine.

I played violin through the first year of college, until I no longer had enough practice time to play at the advanced performance level. Through persistence, I had learned to multitask by concentrating on the notes on the page and the action of my fingers at the same time. With confidence that I could do anything, my desire to excel only grew. In high school, I wanted to join the honors English class, but the head of the department said my standardized test scores were not good enough. I made As in lower-level classes and finally convinced the department to let me try the honors class. I thrived there, breaking the stereotypical test-score barrier set by the school.

Throughout my education, I knew I was capable of a lot more than my test scores dictated, and I would not be content in that box. In my junior year of high school, my parents had a new psychoeducational evaluation done. The psychologist told them that I was placed in a curriculum that was over my head, and that I could not get into a competitive college. Through my fight for the right to try difficult tasks, I developed the ability to be tenacious in my self-advocacy. The college application process, therefore, was very stressful because I best advocate in person, and none of the schools to which I applied gave applicant interviews. I knew my paper applications did not truly reflect my qualifications to be a good college student and was disappointed when the University of South Carolina wait-listed me. Fortunately, the University of Maryland saw through the scores and accepted my early admission! I faced another challenge. Maryland was too big for me, I was advised, but I knew I could beat the odds and succeed there.

I sometimes have had to compromise. I applied to the Business School at Maryland and was disappointed to be accepted for enrollment only at the commuter campus. I wanted to be on the main campus, but I decided no one was going to stop me from going to business school. I accepted the offer, and it turned out to be a good thing. All my business classes were small, but I had the same professors who taught on the main campus, and I received the same degree as students there.

Math has never been one on of my strengths, and today I take a long time to complete reports that contain a lot of numbers, but I have learned to manage by asking questions and accepting help. Internally, however, I always strive for more independent success.

I graduated from the University of Maryland in May 2016 with a degree in international business, and am presently employed by Hilton Worldwide. I continue to advocate for myself. In fact, after four months with Hilton, I received a promotion. Advocating for myself, I told the management that they would regret their decision if they did not choose me for the advanced position.

My advice is do not take no for an answer! If you know you can do something, don't let anyone tell you that you can't. Using your growth mindset, you will find a way to be successful at any task. No matter how many obstacles are put in your path, if you persevere, you will succeed.

—Rose

LEARNING TO LEARN WITH DYSLEXIA

The hallmark phrase "go for it" came to me from my father and has been my lifelong motto, but it has not been an easy standard to meet. At every step, I had to recommit to the goal and the hard work required to attain it.

When I was six, my IQ was tested. My parents, despite both graduating from public school, decided to send their children to private schools, and those applications required IQ scores. Mine reflected superior intelligence, and I was subsequently admitted to what is generally considered the most prestigious private school in Atlanta.

When I entered pre-first grade, this private school ranked me at the top of the class. When I left six years later, my name was near the bottom. By fourth grade, it was clear to me that I was different. I read more slowly than other students. I studied harder, had tutors, and yet did not excel. Most of the other students in my class did not receive outside instruction as I did, but even with the extra help, I was not performing to my full potential; I was struggling.

In fifth grade, my math teacher took it upon herself to grab my worksheet and proclaim in a voice loud enough for the entire class to hear that not only was my work incorrect but I had failed to keep up with the rest of the class. I started crying and left the room. This made a dramatic scene. My math teacher found me in the hall, sobbing with embarrassment and feelings of inferiority. Being escorted back into that math class was humiliating. I held my head low and felt my self-esteem evaporating. The frustration had become intolerable. I remember hurting because I had disciplined myself to make great efforts but had failed to achieve the desired results.

Fortunately, I am blessed with loving parents who always placed the well-being of their children first. My mom and dad recognized a change needed to be made. By God's grace, Mom and Dad discovered Selma Ridgway and Woodward Academy's Transition Program. I distinctly remember being interviewed by Mrs. Ridgway in her office. We talked about my current outlook on education and my present daily academic experience. She decided to accept me into Woodward's Transition Program, and my life immediately began to change. Mrs. Ridgway recognized that I was dyslexic, which was confirmed by outside testing. It was a relief to be told that nothing was wrong with me. I simply had a different learning style. Interestingly, learning basic concepts presented a challenge, but my retention and application of those concepts were exceptional and consistent with my IQ score.

I remain grateful that Woodward Academy uncovered my different learning style. During my time there, I was taught how to learn with my dyslexic mind. In seventh and eighth grades, Jane King taught me English. Her class and instruction put my life on a productive, upward trajectory that lasts to this day. Mrs. King emphasized the importance of reading while simultaneously thinking critically about the subject matter presented. What is the main idea? Why is the author writing this story? Who are the important characters?

Mrs. King instilled in me the urge to read actively, think critically, and reason with logic. She also recommended I read my written assignments backward to proofread effectively. Mrs. King rewarded hard work. There were no unearned rewards. I knew this because she also taught honors English. In many respects, Mrs. King's Transition Program English course was more demanding than the prep classes in middle school. If I could succeed in Mrs. King's classroom, I concluded, I could succeed in any academic environment.

In eighth grade, I approached Mrs. King about setting the goal of earning an exemption from final exams. Woodward allowed students to skip finals if they had a minimal cumulative grade point average (GPA) of 3.2. To achieve this GPA, I would have to earn an A in her class, but Mrs. King explained that the Transition Program was not designed to give high grades. This program's mission was to teach students with different learning styles how to approach academic coursework and prepare for collegiate and life success. However, she made a deal, a contract, with me that, if I were to do the work to meet her halfway, she would ensure I had the tools to reach my potential.

In the classic legal sense, we had a meeting of the minds. Mrs. King and I spent a lot of time together. She gave me individual instruction. If certain techniques did not work, we would try a new approach. We never gave up on each other. We both worked hard and were resilient. I trusted Mrs. King and her instruction, and in eighth grade, I earned the GPA required to be exempt from final exams. At the time, I called this *being in eighth-grade mode*. I resolved that nothing would prevent me from achieving my goals. Throughout life, I have kept motivating phrases in mind for tackling adversity. Activating *"eighth-grade mode"* is one of my favorites.

The skills learned in Mrs. King's class allowed me to succeed at UGA, graduate from the Georgia State College of Law, pass the Georgia bar exam, and earn a partnership at a large Atlanta litigation law firm. Selma Ridgway, Jane King, and my parents were all indispensable in creating this success. Both my mom and dad discussed substantive course work with me, were engaged in my learning, and encouraged me to set high goals. I'd be coy if I did not state that my belief in God was a critical component of my formula to overcome dyslexia. Without exceptional parents, talented teachers, hard work, and religious faith, I would not today be living a productive life.

When I was a high school senior, Bill Lineberry accepted me into his honors political economics class and his advanced placement (AP) American government course. With the benefit of skills developed in seventh and eighth grades, I earned As in these subjects. Unquestionably, these accomplishments, and Bill Lineberry himself, reinforced my belief that I could achieve my goal of graduating from law school. Everyone needs victories to build confidence. Though the hard work was mine, Woodward's academic standards and teachers not only built my confidence but also gave me a lifelong blueprint for how I learn.

This blueprint ultimately became my strategic plan for tackling life one goal at a time. I reasoned that because I understood how my dyslexic mind worked, I could overcome future adversity. Nothing would be harder than making the transition from my fifth-grade math class to thriving in the advanced-placement American government class. I left Woodward selected by my classmates as Most Likely to Succeed and entered UGA with optimism about myself and the future.

At Georgia, I worked hard and earned a 4.0 GPA in my major, political science. I served on the Academic Dishonesty Board and was inducted into Pi Sigma Alpha (the National Political Science Honor Society) and Omicron Delta Kappa (the National Leadership Honorary Society). In my junior year I was asked to speak on behalf of the UGA student body at the inauguration of

UGA President Dr. Michael F. Adams, with thousands of people from all over the country in attendance. During law school, I gained honors recognition for performance in a mock trial litigation course and "booked" (earned the highest grade) the class in interview, negotiation, and counseling.

As a practicing attorney, I enjoyed success in civil litigation and was selected for partnership at age thirty-seven. I have also chaired the state of Georgia's ethics commission (Georgia Government Transparency and Campaign Finance Commission) and served as deputy legislative counsel to Georgia's lieutenant governor. The foundation for all these experiences began with my parents, the staff at Woodward, and faith in God. Having people who were committed and invested in me, and my development, was critical.

Dyslexia, or any different learning style, is a gift if one is open to perceiving it as such. The secret is to react positively to it, make the necessary adjustments, and learn how you yourself learn. Do that, and your success will amaze you—and others.

—Kevin

SHOW UP EARLY, STAY LATE

I entered the Transition Program at Woodward Academy in sixth grade after a teacher at my former school suggested I get tested for a learning disability. The diagnosis validated her suspicions, noting that I had ADHD and visual language processing problems.

I never took any ADHD medication until age twenty-seven, and then only for a limited time to get through the testing required to enter my current profession. I got one of my highest scores on a test of any kind then, but it wasn't worth my staying on the medication because it completely changed my personality.

I have struggled mightily with reading comprehension all my life, a challenge that held me back in English and history and any class requiring memorization. Woodward was difficult because so much of the curriculum revolved around reading, writing book reports, papers, essays, and memorization for tests. Not one of these skills came easily for me. Fair to say, I was not a good student.

However, tough love from certain teachers at Woodward taught me I could be a better writer, a better learner, and ultimately, a better person. In middle school my English teacher, Jane King, asked the class to write a two-page paper to turn in the next day. Papers were always a struggle for me, and to fill two pages, I usually resorted to increasing font size, squeezing in the margins, and other tricks. But this paper was different. Nearly twenty years later, I can't recall exactly what the subject was, but for the first time in my life, it was something in which I had an interest. I think I turned in an eight-page paper that next day—with standard font and margins.

Later that night, I was in the kitchen when I saw our phone's caller ID display, "KING, WAYNE." This wasn't the first time I had seen that name on the caller ID. I was accustomed to Wayne's wife, Jane, my English teacher, calling about once a month to talk to my mom about how I needed to focus better, how poorly I had done on a test, or some topic related to my grades or behavior. Forty-five minutes after the phone rang, my mom came back in the kitchen to tell me and my dad how excited Mrs. King was about the paper I had handed in that day.

I realized there was hope! It turns out that I actually did have the ability to put my thoughts on paper quite well when the subject was something other than dissecting poetry or explaining literary symbolism.

When a person learns differently, certain aspects of school life are tough. Different groups of students are subjected to certain stigmas, and students in the Transition Program were no exception. I always operated under the assumption that when you are born with certain disabilities, God makes it up with strengths in other areas. I believe it is up to individuals to recognize and capitalize on those strengths and never feel sorry for themselves. I never let negative attitudes related to learning disabilities enter my mind.

> *I always operated under the assumption that when you are born with certain disabilities, God makes it up with strengths in other areas.*

The Transition Program instilled in its students many habits that I still use just about every day in my professional life. Beginning in sixth grade, we were taught the following time management tips during test taking:

1. Read over the entire test before you answer any questions.

2. Always complete the easiest part of the test first, while you are fresh. This also gives you time to think about questions from the difficult portions of the test.

3. Review your answers from the entire test before you turn it in.

How could I ever forget these principles after Mrs. Coleman engrained them in our brains? Even though I had extended time on most tests in high school and college, I used these rules, which as I mentioned, I continue to use today. For example, I outline all important e-mails, write them in draft format, print them double-spaced, and then proofread and edit them before hitting "send." If need be, I will edit them from my phone at home before I send them.

I finished Woodward with a sub-3.0 GPA and enrolled in the School of Accountancy at the University of Mississippi in 2003. It's one of the top twenty accounting schools in the country and has a very difficult track, with or without learning disabilities. It was difficult to imagine that I would actually graduate from the master's program, but I was going to try to get as far as possible. My backup plan if I had to withdraw was to apply the course credits I earned to a related but easier subject, such as finance.

I required one-on-one tutoring from my sophomore year through my graduate year of college to get through accounting classes. The lecture format of college courses was a whole different ballgame from the almost personal attention of the smaller class sizes which I enjoyed in high school.

College was a rude awakening, but I attacked the five-year master's program one day at a time. This is one of the greatest lessons to carry through school and into the professional space. I gave it my all every day so nothing more could be expected of me.

It wasn't until the fourth year of college that I realized I could do well in classes I actually had an interest in—for instance, a real estate class. Big life lesson here: do what you enjoy and your success will be much easier and the workload more tolerable. I still remember seeing the similarities between this real estate class and that essay I wrote for Mrs. King's class in middle school: when you have a subject that you can relate to or that you enjoy, you will find that writing eight pages about it comes much easier. I filed this mental note away for life after I graduated.

I ended up graduating with a master's in accountancy. I was at the bottom of my class but miles ahead of the many students who began that journey with me in the freshman year and dropped out because they couldn't pass certain classes. I was not discouraged about barely graduating from this program; I was elated to have completed such a difficult journey.

Throughout my four years in the School of Accountancy, many of my fellow students used the same study areas I did to do homework. I was usually the first one to show up and the last to leave. Often, tests were handed out in order, from the highest grades to the lowest. Invariably, my grade ranked toward the bottom of the pile. I always found solace in the saying, "Do you know what they call the guy who graduates top of his class from med school? A doctor. Do you know what they call the last-placed guy in his class? A doctor." I would rather be the guy who finished last but pushed himself and learned a great deal about the subject and himself than be the guy who chose the easy subject and course load.

I learned in my first accounting class that I did not want to be an accountant, but I operated under the premise that this background would serve me well in the business world, and that was what I wanted after graduation. Classes were grueling and there was almost always one, if not two, classes each semester that I wasn't sure I could pass. A failing grade meant I couldn't continue on this path. Changing my major to a general business field such as marketing would have been easy. Many fellow students did this, but I didn't. I held to a lesson I learned in middle school when I came home early after quitting the wrestling team one day and my father told me that I needed to finish what I started.

In fact, my desire to quit the wrestling team had a lot to do with my learning disabilities. In wrestling, there are dozens and dozens of moves that you use against your opponent. We were shown each move once or twice and then expected to remember it. That's not how my brain works. I have a very difficult time learning visually. I have to use what I am learning; often, I have to do something several times to learn it. The frustration of not being able to learn the moves as quickly as others, followed by criticism from the coach, was too much for me to bear. But I was forced to stick with it and, ultimately, became a much stronger person for it.

The completion of a master's degree in accountancy taught me that with a lot of hard work, I could do anything I put my mind to. We are talking about a very difficult achievement for someone who had never accomplished much of anything, academically. What better proof is there that with dedication and hard work, anything is possible? This lesson would serve me well as I entered the business world three years later.

Operating under the premise that to be happy, people must enjoy what they do, I decided a career in sales would afford me the opportunity to work in any number of fields and cater to my need for freedom and my sense of independence, common traits of people with

ADHD. I took all I had learned in my accounting classes and chose a sales field that is heavy on banking and finance. Accounting is different from banking and finance, yet all three fields share many of the same fundamentals.

As with my journey through the School of Accountancy, I had no clue what I was about to get myself into. I decided a career in bond sales checked all the boxes I wanted, and off I went. The success ratio for a bond salesman is very low. Very few survive and even fewer see true success, but this career seemed, to me, to suit someone with learning disabilities, ADHD, and an understanding of how balance sheets and income statements work. I was on my own schedule and not tied to a desk or meeting schedules set by others.

Bond selling is also a field where you eat what you kill and where hard work pays dividends. I thought, and it proved true, that my tendency to be the first one at the library and the last to leave would pay off. In the nearly five years since I started in bonds, I've seen some very smart guys and girls try their hand at this business. They score very well on the exams and think they will have smooth sailing from then on, but many don't do well. I didn't excel immediately, but I was accustomed to showing up early, leaving late, and working harder than others, which positioned me well for this career. It took several years of keeping my head down and grinding it out, but the success I've experienced since then has been great.

Today, I take pride in my accomplishments. I have been blessed beyond my wildest dreams, and that success is all the sweeter when I think back to the stigma associated with the Transition Program students. It is a great feeling knowing that while my grades and struggles throughout high school and college indicated one path, at age thirty-one, I'm living a very different story.

Until recently, my greatest achievement in life was the master's degree I earned in accountancy at the University of Mississippi, yet it is Woodward and the teachers in its Transition Program that I have to thank. The University of Mississippi made it possible, but my Woodward education taught me the building blocks and learning skills that it took to earn both the bachelor's and master's degrees.

To sum up, the following principles got me where I am today:

- Always finish what you start—a lesson I learned at Woodward in seventh grade.

- Give it your all every day—that is the most anyone can expect of you. My father's positive encouragement got me through the toughest classes in college.

- Get outside your academic and physical comfort zones on a regular basis. You will be surprised what you can accomplish.

—William

FAILING TO FULBRIGHT

I will never forget two memories that highlight my learning differences. The first incident occurred on the school bus on the way home. I played the clarinet in the middle school band, and after practice, I was supposed to break down the instrument and put the pieces in their designated spaces in the case. I can't now remember why—maybe I was in a hurry or didn't think it was important—but I usually just tossed the pieces in the case and jammed it shut. As I jumped on the school bus on this day, the case popped open and the clarinet parts tumbled into the aisle. I scrambled desperately to put the pieces in their proper places, close the case, and get out of the aisle so others could board. A classmate of mine snidely commented, "No wonder you are in a special learning program at school."

The second incident occurred in my high school English class when I received the grade of F- on an English grammar test. After class I approached the teacher and asked if there was even such a grade as F minus. I was certain a solid F was the lowest grade a student could get. She replied that for my poor work, there certainly was such a grade. I would never make it in college, she added.

Despite such events during my secondary education, I was fortunate. For the most part, I had teachers who understood my learning issues. I attended a school for dyslexic children where I discovered my strengths and weaknesses. I was given the tools and accommodations to help me learn best, and I was taught how to advocate for the things I needed. And I recognized that despite my difficulties packing a clarinet or remembering grammar rules, I had (and still have) strengths that set me apart from my peers. I hope no students with learning disabilities are left wondering if they are just dumb or lazy. I hope all children realize that they will mature at their own rates—some a bit more slowly than others—and that there is nothing in the world they can't achieve.

Contrary to my teacher's belief, I successfully completed college, graduating with honors, and was awarded a prestigious scholarship to live abroad and teach English. I am now pursuing a career in finance. I am extremely grateful for the support and understanding of my many mentors along the way. My small success is due in large part to their guidance.

—Matt

CHEERED BY SOCIAL SKILLS

My kindergarten teacher called a conference with my parents at the midpoint of the year and told them something was wrong with me. I was not learning like the other children. Once the teacher had decided I could not learn, she ignored me while she taught the other students. My parents made arrangements to enroll me in a special school the following fall. Fortunately, the teacher at my new school understood how to teach children who learn differently. She took me under her wing and challenged me to grow as a student. The learning climate in that school was so positive that I never wanted to leave.

> *Once the teacher had decided I could not learn, she ignored me while she taught the other students.*

My warm fuzzy school, however, said I needed a less specialized academic institution. My parents transferred me to Woodward Academy, where I enrolled in its Transition Program. The teachers were caring, but I missed the warmer, safer climate of my old school and felt lonely as I struggled to keep up. Through the last two years of elementary school and my middle-school years, I worked as hard as I could. I tried all the learning strategies my teachers suggested. Nothing worked. I kept making the same low grades. To make matters worse, in eighth grade, I was diagnosed with severe scoliosis and had to have back surgery. I still struggled academically, and now I had to face the news that my physical activity would always be limited. My dream of becoming a cheerleader seemed forever squelched.

About this time, my parents decided that a new psycho-educational evaluation might provide helpful insights into my learning. I took the tests, and my parents went in for a consultation with the psychologist, looking for new ways to help me. Their hopes were crushed when the psychologist told them to get me out of Woodward Academy, insisting that the curriculum was too hard for me. The same psychologist said we could forget about college; I simply was not college material. Fortunately, my parents believed in me more than in a bunch of test scores.

In high school, I did not want to give up my dream of cheering, and defying the doctor's assessment, I began to privately train as a cheerleader. I was not allowed to join the school squads until my junior year, when the cheerleading coach finally invited me. At last I was doing something recognized by my peers, and I belonged to a group. Whether this success was responsible or my brain growth just caught up with the demands, I began to excel in my academic work, and more important, to believe in myself.

When asked how I survived the years of struggle, I cannot put my finger on any one thing that gave me the courage to persevere, but I never gave up. My parents never lost faith in me. They always told me to do my best and that they would be proud of me. Also, I am told that I never lost my cheerful countenance. I came to class with a smile and never lost my love of people. In other words, my interpersonal skills were strong enough to keep me going. When I graduated from high school, I won the Selma Ridgway Award, given to the student the faculty determines has best used the school's strategy-based instruction and support. Receiving this award made me very proud because it validated my belief that I always do my best.

When it came time to find a college, I discovered that I had also developed strong intrapersonal skills. I knew myself well. I chose the University of Arizona because the school has a program called SALT (Strategic Alternative Learning Techniques) designed to help students who learn differently. I applied and was lucky enough to get in. I have now completed my first year, earning all As and Bs. Through the SALT program, I have a personal advisor who has encouraged me and helped me to keep my academic work on track. As a communications major, I'm hoping to use my interpersonal skills in a career in special event planning. I will be forever grateful to my parents and those teachers along the way who believed in me enough to never give up.

—**Brooke**

CHAPTER 4

FOLLOW YOUR DRUMMER

How does someone "follow her own drummer?" The first step is hearing the beat of the drum. What does it say? Once she hears it, she must have the courage to accept the call, which often points to an unconventional or less-than-obvious plan for a productive future.

In this chapter, contributors reveal both the ability to hear their own beats and the courage to follow its rhythm. The ability to hear is sometimes called intrapersonal skill or self-knowledge. Knowing and admitting what speaks to the heart is crucial. Andrew, a successful actor, knew he could not sit still for an extended period of time; he knew he loved enter-taining people; and he knew he needed a college that would connect most of his courses to his creativity. Grounded in that self-knowledge, he had the courage to settle in Philadelphia, where work was constant, though maybe not as glamorous as in New York. The textile artist, Isobel, never stopped seeking what fulfilled her. As Andrew did, she realized that she was only happy when creating, and she wanted to make others happy through her chosen art. After many detours, she is finally doing just that: helping others solve the "puzzle of art" in their homes with her creative wallpaper and fabric designs. Through the years of testing other routes, she never lost the drumbeat in her heart.

The education administrator—Selma Ridgway—listened to her heart too. Following the beat of her drummer meant helping others find and follow theirs against the odds of conventional wisdom and education. That inner beat proved stronger than the sage advice that particular degrees or a prescribed beat are needed to succeed and make a difference.

BURNING PANTS

Finding my calling in high school now seems a matter of fate, but at the time, luck played its part too. I always loved making people laugh and as a teen, did imitations of everyone from Bill Cosby to Eddie Murphy. Taking an acting class never occurred to me, until I realized that a girl in whom I was interested was taking one. I signed up purely to get to know her and wound up falling in love—with acting.

My dad is in law. My mom taught French and worked as a photographer. Those are great fields, but once I was bitten by the acting bug, I knew I had to follow my own passion. Getting through school and starting a career can be tough for anyone. Someone with ADD and dyslexia—I have both—faces additional challenges, which makes pursuing the thing you love all the more important. It's amazing the strategies you can learn and apply, the obstacles you can overcome, when you're marching to the beat of your own drummer.

In elementary school, I transferred to Woodward Academy, which had a Transition Program for students with learning differences. I had my share of ups and downs academically. Things would be going along great, and then suddenly, a failing grade would appear for English. I normally did fine in English. What happened? Well, the teacher had given an assignment to write an essay for a college application, and since my college of choice didn't require an essay, I didn't think I needed to do it. My literal thinking had gotten me in trouble again.

Assignments that others could complete in one hour might take me two. Getting my homework done required discipline and a realistic time estimate, two things I worked on at Woodward and still rely on every day. The strategies I adapted to my learning style also helped me in theater. I got into a production of *Noises Off* at Woodward and was soon taking classes at a local company in Atlanta, called the Academy Theater.

I chose Adelphi University when it was time for college because the school had a good learning disability (LD) support program and a good school of drama. I wanted a college that offered both support for my disability and a good curriculum in the field I was passionate about. At Adelphi, I would not have to put off focusing on theater for a year or two while I fulfilled requirements and took unrelated general classes. I took exactly one general academic class a semester. The rest of my credit hours—90 out of 120, in fact—were in theater.

Equally important at Adelphi was the fact that every other week I met with a coach. This person provided personal support, kept me apprised of available resources, helped me plan, and was instrumental in my staying on track.

After college, I began acting in Philadelphia, thinking my residence there would be temporary. Of course, the thing to do in theater is go to New York. That's where many of my friends went, but I noticed over time that they weren't getting steady work, and they had trouble getting enough to eat. I met the woman I would later marry in Philadelphia (we now have a thirteen-year-old daughter), and I had plenty of opportunities there. So, once again, I marched to the beat of my own drummer and decided to stay.

As I write this, I've been acting in Philly for nearly a quarter of a century. I've worked in a variety of theaters, including Arden Theatre, Walnut Street Theatre, Phila-delphia Theatre Company, and Wilma Theater. I've won five Barrymore Awards, and I've acted everywhere from Louisville to Cape May to—yes, of course—New York. Earlier this year, I played Lennie in *Of Mice and Men* when the production traveled to Milwaukee after a record-setting run in Philadelphia.

I still have ADD and dyslexia, and I always will. I still take medicine as needed, and I still struggle with certain things. A store I pass every day sells a brand called

Brunig Paints, and I still see "Burning Pants" when I glance at the big advertisement.

> *I still can't sit down and do one task for an hour. Things that take other people one hour take me two. I have to break things up into blocks of time to get anywhere—and that's just fine.*

I still can't sit down and do one task for an hour. Things that take other people one hour take me two. I have to break things up into blocks of time to get anywhere—and that's just fine. One of the things that made me successful was knowing myself, the ways I learn, and what works for me. I have developed the discipline to block out the time I know it will take me to learn my lines for a performance. Since I do four or five shows a year—each lasting seven or eight weeks—that's important.

Being on stage is the perfect job for me in one way because the work changes every few weeks. It's also a challenge because staying focused requires extra effort. If I'm not spot-on and paying close attention to what's happening onstage, I'll start making a grocery list in my head.

Anxiety also has been an issue at times. I learned breathing and physical exercises that help ease that pressure, and training in improvisation has made a difference there too. Unlike actors in some theatrical communities, actors in Philadelphia pride themselves on knowing their lines when they show up for rehearsal, so I wouldn't dare arrive at the theater without being "off book," as we say, on day one.

A support community—whatever form that takes—can be a major help for someone who learns differently. The other things I've highlighted that proved key to my success were following my passion and choosing a school with not only a strong curriculum in my area but also a strong LD support program (for me, the personal coaching at Adelphi was invaluable). Finally, knowing myself—how I learn and how much time and discipline I need to accomplish tasks—became the foundation on which everything rests.

—Andrew

ALIVE WHEN CREATIVE

I knew that I had problems with learning as early as kindergarten, when I couldn't keep up with the other students. At the time, I attended a school in Maryland, and the faculty there told my mother they couldn't help me. They didn't know what to do with someone who learned differently. My mom had experienced similar learning issues as a child and, fortunately, knew exactly what to do. She helped me compensate for my learning differences by honing in on my strengths: art and sports.

I attended the University of Denver for a year, and my grades were okay, but I did not like the school. It was too small and didn't offer many artistic opportunities. Knowing I had to get out, I set my sights on UGA and didn't divert my gaze—I knew what I wanted and needed. I had started taking ceramics in high school and continued working in that medium in college. I realized that art was the only thing that made me happy, and I knew that UGA had a good art school.

UGA also was a much bigger school, and that appealed to me, since I was always trying to prove to myself that I didn't need small classes. I could and I would keep up! Once I transferred to Georgia, I began working with fabric, and something clicked. I knew I probably could not make a living doing ceramics, so I reflected on why I loved that medium so much. It was very hands-on. The material was malleable. I could etch on the surface, paint it any color … Fabric offered all of those qualities and more, so, maybe, this was my real medium. I pursued a degree in textile design, and one of my professors became an invaluable mentor.

I moved to New York after college and got a job working for a jewelry designer, who allowed me to do an apprenticeship with Isabelle de Borchgrave, an artist in Belgium. It wasn't a great fit, but I sure learned to take responsibility for myself, living abroad. My boss knew I was miserable and kept asking me what I wanted to do. After experiencing Isabelle's passion and endless creativity, I couldn't imagine living any other way when I returned to New York. I knew then that I had to begin living my own passion.

The only thing in the world that makes me come alive is being creative. I knew that much, but I wasn't sure how to turn it into a career. Through various jobs, I continued to make art and textiles and, thanks to social media, to share and promote a part of myself that I couldn't during the workday. That sharing on social media platforms led to commissioned projects that gave me confidence when the time came to really go for my dreams.

> *The only thing in the world that makes me come alive is being creative.*

It didn't happen overnight, but after settling on the right medium, I found ways to channel it into a business. I realized I wanted to help people with designs for their homes—on wallpaper, draperies, upholstery. I love working with colors, sizes, and styles, and this came to seem like the perfect outlet for my creativity. I found a manufacturer in New York to produce my wallpaper and a fabric house to make my fabric. As I write this, I've just launched my first fabric collection (my designs can be seen online at www.isobelpmills.com).

I love to create and use my hands. Art is one big puzzle that you constantly must solve through scale, color, shape, orientation. This is what I love about design: the challenge and fun of the endless puzzles.

I've always loved art, always, but I didn't discover fabric design until I was enrolled in my second college. Several jobs and years later, I found a way to produce and sell my own wallpaper and fabric. Finding the right medium—whether you're an artist, actor, or accountant—can take time, but follow your passion, and you'll eventually get there.

—Isobel

PULLING THE PIECES TOGETHER

"Will you serve as the counselor for the students in the ISP program?" With those words, Woodward Academy's headmaster, Don Woolf, changed my life forever. My answer was yes—but no. I said yes because I very much wanted to serve as a friend to the special students in the Individualized Study Program (ISP), but the headmaster had told me the program would not have a director, and I knew that a single counselor could not do the job.

I knew the students needed an administrative advocate; I knew their teachers needed support and occasional guidance in understanding the different learning styles they encountered; I knew parents needed help in understanding how their children learned. My saying yes to the counselor job would have meant there would be no director to fulfill the other roles. The day after his offer, Mr. Woolf came to see me again and asked if I would serve as the director of the program. Hearing the beat of my drummer more loudly than the voice of reason, I enthusiastically said yes, though at that point, I would have been hard pressed to define *dyslexia*. I believed, however, that students' needs could be met with a combination of self-knowledge; knowledgeable, flexible, and caring teachers; a supportive administration; and loving, supportive parents. My job would be easy, I thought. All I had to do was pull together the pieces.

I immersed myself in learning: observing classes, listening to students, reading, and attending conferences. I studied the latest pedagogical approaches. Fortunately, some influential parents grasped the value of the program that was designed to help their different learners and began to provide extra financial support for purchasing cutting-edge teaching materials, sending teachers to conferences, and bringing in outstanding speakers to talk to faculty, administration, and parents. Before long, we heard rumblings about new computer programs designed to augment the learning of special-education students. I attended one of the earliest conferences on using technology to enhance the learning process for students who have disabilities. The cutting-edge programs and methods on display offered possibilities so exciting that I could have flown home without an airplane. I knew it would be morally wrong to deny the students in the special program this assistive technology. With the help of the school administration and supportive parents, we had a laptop learning program for the students in what we now called the Transition Program, years ahead of its time.

Like assistive technology, Woodward too evolved over the years. When I became director of the program for special students, it included one section of combined fourth and fifth-graders, one section of sixth-graders, and students in the seventh to tenth grades, many of whom split their schedules between special and main-stream classes. Through word of mouth that our special learners were succeeding, we soon expanded to two full sections each for the fourth, fifth, and sixth grades. We maintained special classes in Woodward's middle school, allowing students to enjoy mainstream classes in their strong subjects, and we eliminated all special classes in the high school. The administration estab-lished an accommodation policy in accordance with the Americans with Disabilities Act, and teachers took special workshops designed to help them incorporate helpful teaching methodologies. Students learned to advocate for themselves and took their rightful places as sports team captains, cheerleaders, performers in school plays, and scholars in AP classes in their strongest subjects.

I have always believed that there is power in knowledge, even knowledge that's tough to accept, and I never minced words about the difficulties children faced in Woodward's challenging college preparatory curricu-lum. I believe that all children can be successful, but sometimes, their success does not come when expected. Lagging behind peers in academic work can be more devastating for students' self-esteem than changing to a setting that matches their maturity level and skill development. Another early and valuable lesson I learned was that standardized tests do not reflect the abilities of special students. Most tests aren't designed for different learning styles, and they don't measure the strength and determination of the human spirit. Denying placement in higher-level classes because of test scores, I realized, was to deny children opportunities to excel in areas of talent.

> *Denying placement in higher-level classes because of test scores, I realized, was to deny children opportunities to excel in areas of talent.*

As the years passed at Woodward—26 in all for me, 24 as director—the Transition Program continued to grow and the administrative duties increased. I loved my job, but I longed to partner with the children to help them navigate the waters of a world that does not always understand that *different* does not have a negative connotation. To hear children accused of not caring about their academic work, of being lazy, or even worse, dumb, broke my heart. I wanted to work with those who have enormous potential, though it might not appear in conventional ways, and who often discover that their greatest strengths lie in their differences. I trained as a strengths coach, learning a language of strengths and nonstrengths to describe the wide variety of human abilities and challenges. I spent 18 months learning to be a life coach and quit my job at Woodward Academy to start Ridgway Coaching.

Throughout the journey, I have been privileged to stand on the shoulders of giants. Administrators and dedicated teachers taught me more than I thought I could learn, and the students and parents shared themselves, their immense knowledge, wisdom, and courage. I am indebted to many for being the wind beneath my wings, but most of my energy and inspiration has come from the students and adults I have known and been blessed to work with.

—Selma Ridgway

CHAPTER 5

MANAGING WITH STRENGTHS

A t the end of a math quiz, I asked students to write down their top three strengths. Most of the papers I collected listed one or two items, and some listed none, an unfortunate result but not a surprising one. When Gallup was developing its Strength Finder instrument, its experts discovered that, as a society, we do not have a language for strengths. A self-help industry has mushroomed around notions of correcting weaknesses, but little attention is paid to developing strengths. If a student who has a learning disability has not discovered a talent in art, music, or sports, he or she often feels devoid of innate gifts of strength.

Sam B, the former Navy SEAL, who starts this chapter, found that his ability to multitask helped him beat the odds in SEAL training and stand among the tiny percentage of sailors to finish the course on schedule. His ADD, seen as a weakness when he was in the classroom, became a strength. In "No Time for Fun," Clinton notes that, as a boy, he was too busy with tutors and extra help sessions to discover his strengths, though he later found that he excelled in the outdoors—and in class, once the material related to business. Sarah, who wrote "Motivated by Passion," struggled so much in school that she took a year off. That space led to her discovery of a passion for children who have autism and to the graduate program now training her to be a behavior therapist. Lee, an executive of a commercial real estate brokerage division, discovered the importance of self-knowledge and learned to use his strong interpersonal skills and available resources to work through areas where he was less strong, using strengths to manage nonstrengths. He discovered his interpersonal skills and found that they were an asset in all walks of life.

HOW ADD HELPED SEAL THE DEAL

Of the 360 men who started in my US Navy SEAL class, eleven progressed straight through the program to graduate from the third and final phase together. Others, who suffered injuries, failed a test, or didn't make some other cut, got rolled back into the following class and graduated later, but the overall attrition rate was still about 80 percent.

People are often shocked by these stats. Why would anyone want to go through such a tough program? They're even more shocked when they hear that I had learning issues in school and was diagnosed with attention-deficit disorder. How can anyone with ADD make it as a Navy SEAL?

The answer to both questions is rooted in self-awareness, something I have focused on from a young age, partly because of the challenges I faced. I had hearing issues as a boy, and auditory testing was the start of an early focus on me, my mindset, and the ways I learned best. I attended terrific institutions, the Atlanta Speech School and then Woodward Academy. The Teachers at these schools helped me grow in self-knowledge, and I began to understand myself—learning me—and backing away from the recommended routes.

I had higher math and science scores on the SATs, so I declared a major in engineering, but I soon realized history was a better fit. Big on organization, I always had to have a list and write stuff down or it wouldn't get done. I was a procrastinator—I still am—and I learned that this was okay. To this day, I procrastinate until the last minute and then the fear of failure —*Oh my god, this is not going to get done*—motivates me.

In a traditional school structure, my ADD could be limiting. I struggled to make myself study, but I noticed that when I was interested in the subject matter, I had no problem. This was why I switched to history. I was fascinated by the Civil War and World War II and did better in school once I focused my studies on some of America's major battles.

This led to another important self-discovery. When I was interested in something, my ADD could become an advantage. My mind worked differently and when my fellow students and I were challenged to come up with theories or solutions, I did not follow the textbook. My answers were often wild, not just outside the box but nowhere near it. That kind of thinking worked for me as a Navy SEAL too. In fact, it's what has always made special operations so successful: the effort of a bunch of guys who think differently and find creative solutions.

SEAL training was certainly not the expected route after UVA, but again, I knew myself and realized that an office cubicle was not for me. My dad, a former naval officer, described the SEALs he'd encountered as "nuts," but I had settled on the military, and the more I researched, the more I realized that I would regret not going after the hardest training pipeline. I wanted the challenge and a nonoffice job that served a higher purpose. The SEALs met my criteria, but would I meet theirs?

When I was interested in something, my ADD could become an advantage.

I showed up in Coronado, California, for basic underwater demolition/SEAL (BUD/S) training, which began with *indoc* (indoctrination). Here we learned about the equipment we would use in basic training, how to run an obstacle course, work with inflatable boats, do certain exercises, and so on. By the end of indoc, my starting class of more than 360 had lost seventy or eighty people. The physical challenges are, obviously, intense, especially in the first weeks, until a trainee can get over the hump and find a routine. This was actually something I had learned at Woodward Academy, where the Transition Program emphasized the benefits of routine.

The first phase of SEAL training—basic conditioning—pushes you to the limits of pain and fatigue, and leaves you close to hypothermia. The second phase is dive related. "Pool competency," as the SEALs call it, and begins with drown-proofing exercises. Your hands and feet are tied, and you must control your breathing, heart rate, and other factors as you bob around the pool. To breathe, you have to exhale completely to sink to the bottom of the pool, so that you can push off, rise to the surface, and grab another breath.

That's the easy part.

In another exercise, you are submerged in scuba gear with a swim buddy. You have to take off your rig and put it on him to share oxygen—all with the facemask duct-taped to simulate night conditions. In one final test in the second phase, trainers simulate a surf hit by tearing off your equipment, tying it in knots, and punching you in the gut. Once the air is thoroughly knocked out of you, you must calm down and follow an intricate, orderly procedure, tracing your gear from the facemask down the airline to find and fix any problems. If you touch one thing out of order, you fail.

SEAL training teaches you to manage stress and get comfortable with being uncomfortable, things that people with learning differences encounter at a young age.

SEAL training teaches you to manage stress and get comfortable with being uncomfortable, things that people with learning differences encounter at a young age. Maybe that gave me an edge, but I would be lying if I said I didn't struggle. In training, I would find myself carrying a log with five other guys and hoping my body would give out just so I could fall and rest on the sand for a minute.

That never happened. The body will go much further than the mind thinks it can. SEALs have a reputation for being cocky, but what people usually see is real confidence. SEALs have been pushed so much further than most people that they understand their true limits. They know themselves extremely well, and that gives them the confidence to tackle challenges.

> *SEALs have a reputation for being cocky, but what people usually see is real confidence. SEALs have been pushed so much further than most people that they understand their true limits.*

SEAL training expanded the self-awareness I had cultivated from a young age, and if anything, my ADD helped me in training. The third phase of training involves land warfare and those who get through it move on to parachuting. I lose focus performing the same tasks over and over, so these diverse training blocks were perfect for me. *Okay, you're going to go skydive and learn how to pack parachutes, then you're going to drive vehicles, then you will be shooting, and then you'll study communications and mountaineering …*

I thrived in that environment. I was the quintessential jack of all trades. In fact, once I got the process of packing my parachute down, I began racing my buddies to see who could pack his chute the fastest. We would jump from a plane, land, lay out the chutes, remove twigs and debris, and get inspected at each stage as we repacked. It became a contest, seeing who could go the fastest before the next jump.

I knew that I had to find ways to keep things interesting or I'd get bored and begin to lag. This might sound strange, but ADD kept me engaged. The key was knowing myself well enough to pick a job that I would find challenging and interesting, one I would not get jaded doing.

> *I knew that I had to find ways to keep things interesting or I'd get bored and begin to lag.*

Now, I'm out of the SEALs and once again considering careers. I'm exploring several options, including some work with a former SEAL who became a serial entrepreneur. He has started a highly successful businesses involving everything from appraisal management to trucking to gluten-free beer. He reinvests a lot of his profits into developing new start-ups, which is where I'm helping out. Creating new companies and products meets my need to keep things engaging and not get stuck on one path for too long. It's nice to know that another SEAL has been able to turn a similar thirst for the new and interesting into great success.

—Sam B

NO TIME FOR FUN

I began my formal education in a very demanding private school. Somehow, I managed to make it through the seventh grade, but in eighth grade the bottom fell out. I hit the wall! No matter how hard I tried or how much I studied, I made the same below-average grades. I was miserable, and so were my parents. At the beginning of the tenth grade, they took me out of a school that did not recognize my disability and enrolled me in a boarding school that did. For the first time in nine years, I began to breathe again. I was not smothered with tutors and extra help sessions.

While in the boarding school, I discovered that physical exercise relieved some of my stress. In the afternoons, I could always find a pick-up game of basketball. Playing hard for an hour or two gave me the energy to tackle my academic work. I made it through high school and entered the College of Charleston in South Carolina. There, I discovered the outdoors. The National Outdoors Leadership School (NOLS) backpacking program proved to be a life changer. I discovered that I could do something and be successful. I later fed my new passion by spending a year out West, kayaking and mountain biking. It is amazing how navigating rough waters or puffing up a mountain can clear the head and change the thinking pattern. It definitely put me in the *I can* mode, so different from the years of *I can't* thinking. After the experience out West, I began competing in triathlons. I still do, when I have time. Exercise continues to be my stress reliever.

After I went to work for my current employer, I returned to college to complete my MBA and discovered that academics no longer threatened my self-confidence because I was studying areas of interest. The work I did in the classroom directly related to what I do in the work place. It was amazing how good grades provided the momentum to persevere through long nights of study.

> *It is amazing how navigating rough waters or puffing up a mountain can clear the head and change the thinking pattern. It definitely put me in the I can mode, so different from the years of I can't thinking.*

I currently serve as the vice president of manufacturing for a furniture company that specializes in light fixtures. I travel to the Philippines, India, and China to purchase products, manage the warehouse for which I purchase, and ensure quality control. Believing in supporting others to help them become their best, I spend a lot of my time in the development of my employees. My passion for helping others developed as a result of those years when no one was helping me to grow. The CEO of the company for which I have worked for twenty years believes in developing the potential of his employees and has provided good mentoring for me.

My learning difference is still with me, but I now know how to manage it. I do not trust my memory, so I write notes to keep important things from slipping through the cracks. I have learned over the years that there will be upswings and downswings. The important thing is to keep a positive attitude during the downswings. Persevere, keep moving forward, and there will be a light at the end of the tunnel.

—Clinton Kilgore

MOTIVATED BY PASSION

At Woodward Academy, I earned all As in sixth grade despite my learning differences. I was "mainstreamed" in seventh grade, and this turned out to be a mistake. I thought my learning disability was fixed, but it wasn't. I had trouble completing homework and could not write papers. Academically, I hit a wall and left Woodward after eighth grade. My difficulties persisted in high school, and in college, I still could not write papers. At one point in college, I fell in love with philosophy, but the roadblock of not being able to write kept me from majoring in it. Discouraged, I almost quit school. My life was changed when I started working with children diagnosed with autism. My desire to work with them motivated me to continue my education.

After three different colleges and seven semesters, I gave up, took a year and a half off, and moved back home to Atlanta. I interned at a school for children with autism while working as a live-in nanny for a little boy with special needs. This experience provided the motivation I needed to enter Wheelock College. Realizing that I could make life better for others, help them realize their potential, and smooth their road validated the path I chose.

School was difficult, but my goal of working with children who have autism made all the difference. Another passion appeared unexpectedly after I read a book that turned me on to theater so much that I decided to major in it, earning my bachelor's degree. Through theater, I fell in love with an organization called Hospital Clown. I became a member of the group and will remain one for life, playing with and empowering kids who have been hospitalized.

I used to think that I could never get through a master's program, but a funny thing happened when I studied theater. My passion for the subject built confidence in my ability to write papers. I applied to graduate school, to study in the applied behavior analysis program at Bay Path University, and was accepted. My first semester went well. Writing papers is now a joy because the assignments relate closely to my work.

Currently, I'm taking time off from my studies to work as a dean in a residence hall for students with high-functioning autism at Landmark College. Working outside the classroom nicely balances my academic work. My plan is to finish graduate school and become a board-certified behavior analyst, applying my knowledge and skills to work with children and/or adults who have autism.

The pivotal moment that propelled me forward came when I discovered my love for those who have been diagnosed with autism. My passions revealed that I was stronger than I thought in certain areas when driven by a love for the people with whom I work and an interest in the subject being studied. Over time, my general abilities and focus have improved too. My brain developed in my twenties, so that planning, punctuality, organization, and dependability are no longer weaknesses. Discovering the particular passions that would allow me to make a difference in the lives of others enabled me to build the necessary strengths. It took time, but was definitely worth the wait.

—Sarah

My passions revealed that I was stronger than I thought in certain areas when driven by a love for the people with whom I work and an interest in the subject being studied.

USING STRENGTHS TO MANAGE NONSTRENGTHS

Wanting the best education possible for me, my parents enrolled me in one of the most prestigious private schools in town. By third grade, problems begin to emerge. The teachers said I was not listening to their instruction. I tried hard but could not remember what they told me to do. I was tested and diagnosed with

ADD. With the help of medication, which, unfortunately, subdued my fun-loving personality, I managed to make it through sixth grade. It became obvious, though, that I needed a different learning environment, so my parents enrolled me in a school that had specialized instruction and a curriculum better suited to my needs.

I made it through high school with the help of a caring study-strategies teacher, but I never became excited about any subject or activity. It was just a ho-hum experience. When I entered college, I wanted to be a premed student and go to medical school, but it didn't take long for that dream to crash. Watching the long hours my premed friends spent studying, I knew I could not sustain that level of concentration. I declared a marketing/business-management major and began to find my niche in the acquisition and application of new skills.

Leadership emerged as a strength when I served as a liaison between campus fraternities and the office of the dean of students. The dean relied on me to help with all discipline cases. I had to thoroughly investigate them and represent my fellow students accurately while upholding the standards of the institution.

Throughout my last years of college and in my present position as the executive director of a division of a commercial-real-estate brokerage company, I have learned that success depends on self-knowledge and the use of innate strengths to manage nonstrengths. I know, for instance, that I have to print all important documents to read because I have trouble comprehending information displayed on a screen. I know that I have to see the end of a document before I can muster the energy to go through it one page at a time. I have learned to use available resources, including people on my team who are more talented than I am in particular areas. Discussion with colleagues helps me clarify ideas. I also have learned that there is more than one way to enjoy activities I am passionate about. I could not go to medical school, but I am on the board of the Atlanta Fire and Rescue Foundation, and I ride with an ambulance driver once a month on emergency calls. I also have become very active in helping young people find their passion through Junior Achievement. It has been my pleasure to work with my children and other middle school students, giving them hands-on experience through sustainable education programs.

I persevered through school until I reached a place that spoke to my strength in interpersonal skills. Recognizing my strengths and using them to manage my weaker areas has led to a successful and satisfying life, both personally and professionally.

—Lee Harris

CHAPTER 6

UNLOCKING THE
ENTREPRENEURIAL MIND

I ndividuals with significant learning differences often talk about having to improvise and find creative solutions from a young age, but this experience seems to serve them well, especially in business. Different learners do not hesitate to take risks; in fact, they thrive on risk taking. They are not deterred by failure, and they are wired to think outside the box, traits that have proved invaluable for entrepreneurs and business leaders including Bill Gates, John Chambers, Richard Branson, and the two contributors to this chapter.

Our first contributor, knowing that he could not sit behind a desk all day, tried several options, including real estate, before starting a successful tugboat company, moving barges up and down the mouth of the Mississippi river. He pounced when he saw an exciting opportunity. His advice to aspiring entrepreneurs is: "Do what you want; do what you love; and do it well. Worry about the rest later." Our second contributor, Robert Morris, did not have access to the specialized education, cutting-edge technology, and new strategies that many of our writers were fortunate enough to utilize. Bobby had to figure out his own methods on the fly, and he gives that experience the credit for much of the creativity and perseverance that served him well in starting and running his own company. As we noted earlier in this book, the student who learns differently might be the most successful person in the class.

A RISKY ADVENTURE

According to my parents, I came into the world looking for an adventure, especially one that would require physical activity. I was enrolled in every team sport available at my age level including tennis, soccer, and ultimately, biking. It became apparent early in my school career that the acquisition of academic skills was going to challenge me. In fact, my studies became an avenue of discouragement rather than a source of achievement. After being diagnosed with a learning disability, I faced my first disappointment: having to leave all my friends to go to a special school. When the time came to leave that school, I was again disappointed. I could not return to my old school, but had to go to one that provided instruction tailored to my learning difficulties.

Luckily, I have always had strong interpersonal skills, which allowed me to manage these early disappointments and make new friends at my third school. Not wanting me to feel like a failure, my father continually sought ways for me to excel in athletics. Road and mountain biking became a part of that strategy and a way to carve out quality family time. Everyone in my family became proficient enough to enjoy the sport, but I threw myself into it with my usual determination and vigor, and, in my age group, I came to rank third in the nation for mountain biking.

At university, I was asked to take a semester off. My parents told me I had to find a paying job, so I got creative about looking for one. If I had to sit out a semester, I was going to find something I enjoyed. I was into cars from a very early age, so I got a job at Global Imports BMW. I worked sixty hours a week and thoroughly enjoyed that semester off campus (at least the working part; living at home with my parents—not so much).

That summer I returned to UGA with a focus on *just graduating.* I realized that the sooner I graduated, the sooner I could return to working at something I enjoyed. I always disliked school and knew that would not change. I returned to UGA and graduated fifteen months later. I never looked back.

Finally, I was done with school—the one thing I was never good at—forever! I moved to Washington, DC, with Kristin, my wife-to-be, and with no help from anyone got a job as real-estate analyst at a commercial firm in Virginia. I worked there for a little over a year before getting a job with Capital Automotive Group, again looking for something that interested me. When I worked at Global Imports during my semester off, I learned quite a lot about publicly traded dealer groups (AutoNation, Sonic Automotive, and Penske, to name a few).

I really flourished at Capital Automotive, which offers sale lease-back and financing to dealer groups and car dealers (we helped buy out Nalley Group while I was there). During this time, a few other guys and I started day trading at work during down time, and I ran across

Kirby, a publicly traded barge/tugboat company. This business really interested me. I did not know a lot about it, but already, I liked it more than the real estate and car businesses combined.

In 2005, when I was discovering the barge company, Hurricane Katrina hit New Orleans, Kristin's hometown. The next spring, we went to a wedding in New Orleans, our first time back after the storm, and I was overwhelmed by the destruction. When we returned to DC, I told Kristin that if she ever wanted to move back to New Orleans, Louisiana, the time was now! And that's what we did. I had a job with a real estate developer within six months and moved to New Orleans in July 2006. Kristin and I were not married or engaged yet, but again, we never looked back. I worked with Stirling Properties for a year, building Target and Walgreens stores, and then left to start Magnolia Fleet, a tugboat and barge business, which was the real reason I had moved to New Orleans.

Today we employ more than 120 people and have operations in Louisiana, Texas, and Alabama. There are plenty of times when this work is not easy or fun, but overall, I love what I am doing, and that's the key to life. Do what you want, do what you love, and do it well. Worry about the rest later.

—John

> *Do what you want, do what you love, and do it well. Worry about the rest later.*

THE HUNTER INSTINCT

I was raised in rural America in the 1960s and attended public schools. By the age of ten, I was struggling in school and in life. I had great difficulty reading, writing, and studying. I knew something was terribly wrong, but the teachers were not familiar with ADD in those days. I had attention-deficit hyperactivity disorder (ADHD) and dyslexia, but no one recognized my medical condition. There simply wasn't an awareness of the different ways that people learn and that conventional classroom strategies failed them. Even if I had been diagnosed, however, the rural public school system and my family did not have the resources necessary to treat such a complex problem.

My secondary-school years were humiliating. Everything was a struggle. My fellow students poked fun at me. My mother somehow convinced me I was smarter than any of those other children, but when I went to school, I felt stupid. I remember taking music in the third grade—until my teacher asked me to perform a trombone solo, which meant reading from the music book. I was mortified and of course, couldn't do it. Later, I recall trying to hide when the teacher called me to the chalkboard to solve an algebra problem or to read out loud to the class. At little league baseball games, coaches sent me to the outfield only when our team was way ahead or way behind because of my limited attention span.

Today, we understand so much more about learning dis-abilities and the strategies and technologies that help, but public schools still have scant resources to identify and help their students. Many of those with learning dis-abilities eventually drop out of school, and a high per-centage of them are attracted to the false security of the wrong support groups, including gangs. Some who could succeed with the right help, ultimately, wind up in a lifetime of crime and incarceration. As difficult as my struggles were, I fared better only because I had a caring family and strong faith.

I was recently robbed at gunpoint by a twenty-one-year-old man. I am convinced his problems began when he flunked out of high school with little or no safety net to prevent him from eventually needing to hold a 9 mm handgun to my head to get $100. He now faces two sentences of ten years minimum for my robbery and for another one he committed the next day. There is no doubt that what he did was awful, but could his life have changed if he had had good parents and educational support?

After not making any of the sports teams, I received the break of my life and turned rejection into opportunity when I found a job delivering the afternoon edition of the local newspaper. In those days, you see, running a paper route was the equivalent of managing a small business. It taught me the basics needed in any business. I learned the importance of collecting receivables and opening new customer accounts. This was an early lesson in cash flow, capital allocation, profitability, and return on equity that would be engrained in me for the rest of my life.

My above-average IQ, work ethic, and compensating skills got me through high school, but with my below-average SAT scores, I was one of the very last applicants accepted to our state university. I struggled in college, but using a self-taught strategy I called "read, write, and repeat," memorization, and other approaches to learning, I improvised and finished in five years.

My grades were, at best, average, but an early decision to be a finance major, an area I excelled in, earned me a slot in graduate school and, eventually, an MBA. I left school with a low GPA score but managed to find an entry-level position with a financial services firm. After just four years, I cofounded my own firm. My father convinced me that I should create my own security rather than depend on a Fortune 100 or Fortune 500 company that might offer me a "package" if times were to get tough. So why do many with learning disabilities do so well owning businesses and being entrepreneurs? Thomas Edison's dyslexia was so bad that his teacher sent him home from school and told him never to return! As a child, Bill Gates, one of the wealthiest people in the world, suffered from dyslexia and/or ADHD. John Chambers of Cisco, Charles Schwab of the eponymous brokerage firm, Pete Kight, founder of CheckFree Corporation, and Richard Branson of Virgin Group all suffered from childhood learning disabilities. We're not like Coca-Cola—there's no secret formula—but we do have a commonality: we seem to be wired differently.

Many of us have creative minds. Some of us tried working for someone else but weren't suited to a rigid corporate environment or a boss who stifled imagination. Overcoming or coping successfully with a learning problem gives us the courage, confidence, and the skills needed to start and operate a business. We embrace measured risk while others seem to flee it. Learning differently has taught us that, if at first we fail, we just try again, using the same alternative path mentality that we used in learning. We are courageous and we realize you cannot win if you are afraid to lose. Some of us seem to have extraordinary vision. We catch things others miss. We see around corners and identify problems before they escalate. For us, it's not where the puck is but where it's going. We are constantly reevaluating our business's place in its industry and adjusting our model accordingly. We have the hunter instinct, are opportunistic, and constantly look for new opportunities. True entrepreneurs know in their hearts that if one business fails, they will simply start another, using the intellectual capital acquired from the first one. We welcome the challenge of facing new problems each and every day. Problems become opportunities for those who can solve them, and we seem especially suited to finding solutions. Successful entrepreneurs multitask and seek outside counsel where needed. It has been said that it is not what you do not know that will get you in trouble, but what you think you know that you do not know that can destroy your business.

We tend to have a keen awareness of our limitations and have sought help all our lives. We have a keen sense of urgency and accomplishment. We have a keen sense of attention to details.

Do not tell us, "You cannot do that." We will prove you wrong. We are tenacious and love winning and will outwork the competition. You see, the odds have been against us most of our lives. We have been swimming upstream to make it to open water. Determination and persistence will always be our alpha and omega. A quote credited to Calvin Coolidge perhaps says it best: "Nothing in the world can take the place of persistence. Talent will not; nothing is more common than unsuccessful men with talent. Genius will not; unrewarded genius is almost a proverb. Education will not; the world is full of educated derelicts. The slogan 'Press on' has solved and will always solve the problems of the human race."

> *Do not tell us, "You cannot do that."*
> *We will prove you wrong.*

Thank you, Lord, for giving me my dyslexia and ADHD and the compensating skills to successfully learn differently. This difference has definitely given me the confidence, courage, and determination to allow my reach to exceed my grasp. My disability has created some hardships for me and my family, but it also has contributed to a successful personal and business life, joys that far outweigh any drawbacks.

Every day, I am grateful for my learning difference, and I am committed to doing my part to ease the challenges faced by so many young people. The hardest million I made was the first one. The easiest was the last one. The most rewarding, though, was the one I was able to give away to help the less fortunate. My journey to success could not have been possible without my village. This includes a patient, understanding and supportive family; loyal customers and friends; and of course my Lord, who for some reason, seems to have held me in the palm of his hands.

—Robert Morris

CHAPTER 7

THE POWER OF A VILLAGE

T he village begins at home. Nothing can replace parents who understand the different learner in the family and are willing to work and sacrifice to make sure a child gets the education best for his or her learning style.

Three of the stories in this chapter are told by parents and two are told by people diagnosed with learning disabilities. In three cases, parents and students utilize the resources of an entire village—family members, special teachers, tutors, support groups, programs, strategies, and public school resources—to become successful. In two cases, the task is a work in progress, still drawing on the strength of the village to build what looks like positive outcomes.

Often, these individuals reflect on the immeasurable impact that a special teacher, an understanding parent, an innovative program, or the right school had on their learning and long-term success. Caring parents realize that a dyslexic daughter's acceptance of a new school will make the same transition easier for their dyslexic son. Another parent partners with the public school to map a program for a struggling student. Professors offer extra time during office hours, former bosses provide recommendations, and fellow parents give advice. Professionals administer tests and diagnose differences, a key step in accessing all the village has to offer and understanding that a so-called disability doesn't prevent learning. Often, it simply means extra time and different strategies. As one parent says, "Be prepared for a marathon, not a sprint."

THE POWER OF A VILLAGE

On May 7, 2017, we celebrated with great emotion our son Henley's graduation from Belmont University in Nashville. It was a day that shouldn't have happened, according to the statistics. How can a dyslexic, dysgraphic, ADD student make it through elementary school, let alone college? Such an achievement requires the help of an entire village.

We could share lots of happy and sad stories and endless advice with families facing similar challenges, but our trial-and-error approach to learning differences led to clarity about the importance of certain measures. We'll highlight them below.

Our trial-and-error approach to learning differences led to clarity about the importance of certain measures.

1. **Access resources.** Get the very best experts and special education that you can afford. New science, medicine, technology, and learning techniques are being developed every day, and they can make a huge difference in your child's success. Cutting-edge resources are accessible and affordable. Do your research. Talk to other parents. Join a parent group. Develop a stable of good resources and nurture those relationships.

2. **Identify a passion.** Encourage your children to find and live out their passions. They might not be similar to the interests of anyone else in your family. Be comfortable with different. Embrace it. This will help your children find their life's work and pleasures.

3. **Play as a team.** Your child's learning disability affects everyone in your home. Make sure that both parents are pulling in the same direction and have the same information. Don't unknowingly exclude another student in your home who faces fewer challenges, a common pitfall. Give your child (and yourself) some downtime to reboot.

4. **Work the system**. Special accommodations can make the difference: you child sits at the front of the class, does half the assigned problems, uses a computer and calculator and optical scanning software, and takes personally tailored standardized admissions tests. Maintain an open dialogue with teachers. Most of them really want to help. Bribes of baked goods are sometimes helpful.

5. **Be reasonable.** Go into every class and subject knowing that your child will probably take at least twice as much time to complete assignments. Work with your teachers to edit homework. If high-school students normally spend four hours a night on homework, you (and good teachers)

don't want your child to be spending eight hours. The return is not directly correlated to time spent.

6. **Take a break.** Many students with learning differences succeed in extracurricular activities, gain confidence from them, and make non-LD friends. Think sports, theater, music, photography, outdoor club. Students usually do better, academically, when they are engaged beyond books.

7. **Be patient and smart.** This is a marathon, not a sprint, which is something that's often hard for dads to understand. Change is slow and sometimes impossible. Figure out a way around it. If your child is never going to learn the multiplication tables, move on to the calculator. If your child is never going to be a fluent reader, buy the reading software. It's not about your child's mastering the same techniques as everyone else, but finding the best way for your child to learn.

8. **Teach independence.** Encourage your child to advocate for himself or herself as soon as he or she can. Teachers are more responsive to students than to parents. Have special accommo-

dations written out for each year. Have your child review them with the teacher after-hours. Teach your child to ask for help. Have him or her get to know the disability counselor at college. Send that person baked goods too.

9. **Manage expectations.** It's okay to "cry uncle." Sometimes, the only way your child can make it is to have a tutor, drop a class, take an incomplete test, or fail a test. It's better to teach your child to be realistic about how to solve a problem than to "succeed" in the moment.

10. **Let go and let God.** Get down on your knees every day and thank God that you have a unique child whose accomplishments are all the more cherished for the difficulties he or she has to overcome to succeed.

—Sal and Brad Kibler
parents of Henley Kibler and Bradley Kibler

TIME, HARD WORK, AND A LITTLE HELP

From early elementary school onward, I had difficulty learning. I started in the gifted and talented program in a public elementary school but took a long time to do my homework. When I moved to a private school in sixth grade, the homework hours only increased. Reading and writing were the most challenging. Even though I had tutors to help me learn phonics and used other reading strategies in elementary school, these lessons never stuck. I became good at memorizing words, but the harder school became, the more I struggled. I could not sound out words. I would get confused and not understand sentences.

My learning disabilities were more specifically diagnosed in the seventh grade. I had been tested twice before, in elementary school. By the third time, I practically knew the questions on the tests and remembered the stories. Tests showed that I had the capacity to do well, but I was underachieving.

My grades improved when I began to get a few accommodations, and midway through the first quarter of eighth grade, I changed most of my regular prep classes at Woodward to the Academic Program and Transition Program classes. This would be the last year I could take advantage of full immersion in the Transition classes.

Moving into the Transition Program at Woodward made a big difference for me because instructors taught students in more than one way. I am not an auditory learner. I need to visualize something, see it written on the board, or use kinesthetic learning (using a physical activity, such as writing a lesson down), to retain it. I learned the standard curriculum material in Transition classrooms, but I understood it better because of the way it was taught. The study skills I learned, the tutors who helped me to improve my learning style, and neurolinguistic processing (NLP), a strategy I used to memorize and recall, made a huge difference in my grades.

Using new study skills and NLP, I moved from Cs to As and Bs by the end of eighth grade, doing well enough to be exempted from exams, a huge reward for all the extra hours of studying. Hope for good grades and a successful future returned.

My mom, my tutors, a teacher named Mrs. King, and NLP made my early successes possible. My mom, my biggest cheerleader and supporter, pushed the hardest to identify obstacles and remove them. My tutors in elementary school helped me to sound out words and understand my reading assignments. In middle school, Mrs. King was my hardest teacher. She pushed me to get better, and it paid big dividends. I remember crying on that first day in her class because I was so overwhelmed, but at the end of the year I was smiling because I had come so far. I learned NLP outside school with an education specialist. This memory tool, which allows you to absorb information visually through the brain's input spot, and then recall it by accessing the brain's output spot, was invaluable.

I still can't spell very well, but I have improved; the spell checker is my best friend. Recently, I also have begun using Siri, an app on my phone that lets me ask questions and get the correct spelling.

At Woodward, most classes allowed accommodations, and all the teachers were at least familiar with them. In college, though, I had to be an advocate for myself and my needs to get accommodations. At the beginning of every semester, I set up a time with each professor to discuss my needs for extra time and a different place to take tests.

I also had to get comfortable with my strengths and cater to my optimal learning style by getting extra help when I did not understand what had been discussed in class. I learned that my weakness in spelling has not been as much of a disadvantage in the work force as I had anticipated. Many people have difficulty spelling and have never been diagnosed with a learning difference. If you can make a joke about it, it's not as big a deal to others as you might think.

Leveraging all the skills I learned at Woodward and elsewhere, I wound up representing Clemson in a national competition based on a research paper that I had written. Winning that contest and collecting a two-week, all-expenses-paid trip to visit packaging facilities in Italy was the highlight of my college years. The award opened doors for me in the international industry in which I enjoy working today and was an exponential leap forward, considering my learning challenges.

The idea that everyone learns the same way is a common misconception. When I moved into the Transition Program, I thought I would be with less intelligent students, but I was wrong. Teaching the same subject for different learning styles—visual, auditory, kinesthetic, or various mixtures of these and others—allows students with learning differences to access the material much better and faster.

Once I understood how I learn best, I had to advocate for myself to make sure the teacher would also present the material in a way I could understand. In small and large college classes, I learned to sit in the front of the classroom so that I would not be distracted. I also tried to sit on the right-hand side of the room because my NLP input spot required that I look at things with my eyes slightly to the left. Most people think only the really smart student sits in front. I might not be the smartest person in the room, but I'm smart enough to know my focus will improve according to where I sit.

My greatest accomplishment is earning an MBA from UGA's Terry School of Business. I proved to myself something I thought was impossible. After graduating from Clemson University with a degree in packaging science (a five-year program that included a six-month co-op), I thought I would never take another test or go to school again.

I also never thought I could get into a graduate program. I'm not the best standardized-test taker, and studying for the GMAT took many hours with no guarantee of getting into any MBA program. I thought I would need to be re-tested to prove that I still had a learning disability and needed extra time on that test. By the grace of God, however, I attended a "lunch-n-learn" about the Professional MBA Program at UGA's Terry School and learned that the program sometimes waived GMAT scores if it could rely on the student's college GPA level, number of years of significant work experience, and two letters of recommendation.

I took a chance, wrote my essays, and sent in my resume and transcripts. My current boss and former boss from the previous company were glad to write recommendations. A week later, I received a phone call notifying me of my acceptance into the program, something I never thought possible. Thankfully, they realized that those standardized tests don't show the whole person or what that person can accomplish with hard work.

I had considered the idea of graduate school crazy, but now here I was, getting an MBA and working at the same time. I knew it would advance my career, and fortunately, I was able to use the same accommodations I had used in college: taking tests in a separate room, with extra time. This helped me focus and eased the anxiety I felt when I saw people finish before me.

I graduated with a great GPA and kept my job and my friends. I loved learning new business concepts that I could apply to my everyday job. I was also able to participate in a study-abroad trip, a bonus that had eluded me, as an undergrad, because of the rigorous program.

I'm thankful that I found three exceptional programs: the Transition Program at Woodward, the Packaging Science Program at Clemson, and UGA's Terry School of Business MBA Professional Program. They allowed me to thrive and to prove that with hard work and determination, I can make my dreams come true. They may just take a little longer.

—Virginia

JUST GET HIM THROUGH SCHOOL

When the time came to make the transition from coloring inside the lines to learning how to read, my struggle with dyslexia began. My second-grade teacher told my mother that something was not quite right, and I should be tested. I would come home from school and fight with my mom about doing my homework. I hated school, I hated reading, and I hated homework. Of course, this was all because I comprehended very little of what was being taught. Yelling, screaming, and doing anything I could to get out of homework was a nightly occurrence at home. My mom finally said enough was enough, and we began the testing process.

Most people reading this book understand that being tested for a learning disability is not nearly as simple as a blood test, for which you get the results almost immediately. Testing for a learning disability takes time. The tests showed that I was dyslexic and had ADD and ADHD. While the testing went on, I got special help at the public school I attended. It was the same class that some of the special education students took. Leaving my regular class to go to the "special" class was never easy because I had to explain to the other kids why I went.

In the fifth grade, I entered the Schenck School. I knew this was going to be a special place because, before I even got there, the current students wrote letters welcoming me. Two of the students who wrote letters had left the school before I got there, but two years later, we were all at Woodward together. To this day, we are best friends. Those simple letters meant so much to me; it was such a relief to know that I was about to go to a school where the kids were like me. With ten kids in a class and two teachers, I was finally going to get the help that I so desperately needed.

I owe all of my success in life to a very special teacher at Schenck named Patty McEwen. She saw something in me and took me under her wing. I had the good fortune to have Mrs. Patty for both fifth and sixth grades. At Schenck, the faculty gave us the tools we needed to overcome our learning disabilities, from math tricks to spelling by tracing words and saying them aloud. The teachers taught us to believe in ourselves when so many others had given up on us and moved us to "special" classes. We were all incredibly bright but just did things differently.

After Schenck, I moved to the Transition Program at Woodward Academy. Schenck brought me a long way, but I had a great deal of catching up to do. Let's just say I failed the better part of middle school. I was allowed to stay because I was attentive in class and did my homework, but something was just not clicking yet. After I left Schenck, Mrs. Patty continued to tutor me after school. She would pick me up from the bus with Leo, her huge black lab, and take me to McDonald's. After Leo and I had finished my fries, it was time to get to work.

Knowing that quitting was not an option, I continued on a difficult educational path, and when I got to high school, something clicked. Between Ms. Stephenson's study skills class and Mrs. Patty's tutoring, the fruits of all my hard work began to show themselves. I made the honor roll every year of high school. I learned to never quit and that hard work paid off. After Woodward, I went on to Auburn University, where I graduated with a degree in business administration.

Today I am a financial advisor for UBS Investment Bank in Atlanta and have the good fortune of working with my dad. You never outgrow your disabilities; you find ways to overcome them. Flash cards have turned into sticky notes. When I meet people, I say their names six times to myself to remember them, and keeping a good calendar is critical. People with learning disabilities are not dumb; they just do things differently. Consider Howard Schultz, the founder of Starbucks, or Daymond John, the founder of FUBU. Both have learning disabilities but stayed the course and remained persistent. Look where it took them.

> *You never outgrow your disabilities;*
> *you find ways to overcome them.*

I wanted to do something to give back to the Schenck School and Mrs. Patty, so I started Sporting Clays for Kids, an annual sporting clay-shoot fundraiser to raise awareness of the school and of children with learning disabilities. All of the proceeds raised by the event go into an endowment that allows staff to get the training they need to stay on the cutting edge and help others, just as they had helped me.

Mrs. Patty always told my mom, "If we can get him through school, he will do just fine at life." To my mom and Mrs. Patty, thank you!

—John Curtis Fisher

THE "WRIGHT" PLACE FOR OUR FAMILY

The Wright family is no stranger to learning differences. One of my and my wife's most stressful parts of being a parent was breaking the news to our daughter that she was dyslexic. Our son is dyslexic too, but I knew he would be fine with that news and a school change as long as we sold his sister on her transition.

The anticipation of telling our daughter about her dyslexia was unbearable. She was going to have to leave a school she loved and fight her way through a new one just as I had. I too have dyslexia, and I understand the challenges it can create. We prepared ourselves for the all-out meltdown that would occur when we informed her she would be leaving her old school.

To our surprise, we were met with a calm five-minute conversation in which we informed her that she was dyslexic. This was why she had trouble reading and writing, we explained, and why she would move to the Schenck School, which specialized in educating children with dyslexia.

She told us she was ready to go. She was relieved and wanted to get the help that would make her a great reader and writer. End of the conversation. She never looked back and never questioned why. I am still in shock. She knew that this was what she needed and wanted.

Here is some of the advice I have given to our children about dealing with dyslexia.

1. It's a family tradition: dyslexia, Schenck School, and working hard.

2. You will work 100 times harder than a nondyslexic person to learn the same lesson.

3. Work, work, work harder, and never give up.

4. Try, try, memorize, try again. Repeat.

5. Read. Write. Repeat.

6. Your hard work will pay off, not only today but also when you are older. It will make you stronger.

7. Things might be harder for you today, but one day, you will be able to do things nondyslexic people cannot. Never give up, and you will not be defeated. To this day, the ability to bounce back from setbacks remains the greatest gift that Schenck and dyslexia have given to me.

8. Some go to Harvard and some go to Yale. The Wrights go to Schenck. Then again, you never know.

—Jeffrey

PARTNERING FOR SUCCESS

Partnering with the public schools to meet the needs of a special learner can be daunting, to say the least. In working with the public system to obtain services for my two special-needs children, I have found the following to be helpful:

□ **Research:** Read books on learning disabilities, talk to other parents who are experiencing the same struggle. Review the county website to better understand the process and begin work to obtain a

504 Plan and an individualized education program (IEP). Ask lots of questions and take good notes.

- **Private testing versus public testing:** Your local school can provide an evaluation for free, but this won't be as comprehensive as a private test. You want the school test, to receive the school's services, but you also need private testing to gather more in-depth information in order to understand the disability.

- **Check your child's work:** Sometimes, a 100 is not really a 100; your child's assignment might contain wrong answers. Was the grade given for effort rather than correct responses? If your child is well behaved and a favorite of the teacher, the assessment might go easy on him or her. Go through the papers every week, and if you see incorrect answers, schedule a conference ASAP. Your child is *not* on track.

- **Organize:** Keep a binder with test results, work samples, and milestone tests. You will need this for school meetings or MD appointments.

- **Keep work samples:** Keep some of your child's school work samples to discuss your child's progress with the teachers.

- **Check your child's work against another child's:** As strange as this sounds, ask a parent whose child has the same assignment if you can see that child's work. Explain that you suspect your child might not be held accountable as his or her peers are. If you see your child's work does not match, then you know what to work on.

- **Ask questions of everyone:** If you know teachers, ask them what works and what doesn't. Learn what a 504 Plan and an IEP are and how to get them. Learn how to document your child's progress, to gather the data that the school will need to give your child an IEP or a 504.

- **Stand out/be polite/be firm:** This is your child's future, so you need to "bother" the teacher. It is important to be polite, but plow a path forward if you don't see improvements. There is a fine line between being an advocate for your child and behaving in a way that makes the school play the

"Imperial March" as you enter the building (that's Darth Vader's theme song—you get the picture). Not everyone is going to love you, because you mean extra work.

- **Buy school stuff:** Buy stuff for your children, of course, so they are prepared (teachers really don't like kids who show up unprepared). But more important, buy stuff for the school. Have it delivered directly to the teacher or administrator from whom you need help. Online retailers such as Costco and Office Depot deliver for free. In winter, buy bulk tissues and hand wipes. Pencils also go a long way. Throw in some mints to get free shipping and the front office will love you.

- **Take a partner to meetings:** I learned from my sister, who is a teacher, that the school takes you seriously when both parents show up. They know you mean business, you are working as a team, and it is important to the family that your child succeed. If both parents cannot show up, take a grandparent or friend.

▫ **Take an advocate to meetings:** If you are not sure that you will understand all the school is telling you in a 504 or IEP review, hire a professional who specializes in learning disabilities or knows how to navigate a school system. Schools will want you to disclose, before the meeting, if an attorney will be present.

▫ **Meet once a month, or every other month, with teachers:** This is important so that teachers know you arc bchind your child, can stay up to date, and track progress. Again, be polite but firm.

▫ **Create a team:** This includes teachers, doctors, tutors, babysitters, and so on. All these people can help with your child's progress. It might be stressful to work with your own child on reading and other skills, so find resources to help with this. It will reduce stress and allow you to spend your energy loving your child unconditionally.

▫ **It's not your fault; get over it:** Your children are uniquely made by God. Their learning disabilities were not caused by vaccines, failure to eat enough meat when you were pregnant, not drinking enough milk, or lack of vegetables. Don't waste mental energy on feeling sorry for yourself; it's not about you. Recognize your children's strong suits and foster what interests them and engages them in learning.

▫ **Not everything can be solved by an app:** Don't buy an app and expect your child to learn the letters, numbers, or how to read. Apps are great tools, but you cannot depend on screen time with a child who has a learning disability. Schools love to test using computers, but your child might need an accommodation to read his or her test on paper. Work with your child on using technology and see how he or she performs with it versus paper.

—Blair

CHAPTER 8

NO MANUAL IN THE CRIB
(Voices of Parents)

"Devastated ... I felt the rug had been pulled out from under me ... The earth shifted ... A successful night was one without tears ... I tore up the crib looking for the manual because, I thought, surely my child had arrived with instructions."

These are just a few of the reactions experienced by parents on learning that their precious children had learning disabilities. Realizing that their hopes and dreams for their children require more effort than expected makes accepting a diagnosis difficult.

A couple tells how they were bewildered when they realized their son had to learn how to learn. A mother of two children with learning disabilities explains that she and her husband had to find a new road for their journey. Another mother shares the frustration of a night when her middle-school son tackled demanding homework. Another talks about the necessity of changing schools because her son's fifth-grade teacher did not have a manual that worked for a bright student who learned differently.

In all of these stories, you will hear parents sharing the manuals they had to develop for themselves, each one tailored to a particular child's needs and learning style. Developing those manuals required continual problem solving and improvisation. Parents found support teams that could help and continued solving problems until their children understood their own strengths and weaknesses well enough to manage for themselves.

THE EVOLUTION OF UNSPOKEN DREAMS

As do most parents when they have a son or daughter, I had certain dreams and expectations for my own son and daughter. Many of those dreams were unspoken and could perhaps be best described as things I assumed they would achieve: unlimited success at school, their pick of colleges, easy friendships, and thriving and fulfilling careers. I anticipated the ordinary challenges of raising two children, but also an uncomplicated family life. That was the journey for which I was prepared.

The early clues pointing to the coming detours were subtle: teachers reporting, "She can't remember how to spell three-letter words" or "He can't sit still in class." I heard, "She scores too low on comprehension questions" and "He can't remember the order of the months of the year." Testing confirmed learning disabilities. That's a devastating diagnosis for most parents. It put in sharp relief the fact that my children's paths would be different from those of other children, and, more painful, that my parental expectations needed to be thrown out the window. We would have to find our own path and go on our own journey.

> *As do most parents when they have a son or daughter, I had certain dreams and expectations for my own son and daughter.*

Stumbling is part of the journey. My family made its share of mistakes, but for parents who have discovered recently that their children have learning disabilities, I'd like to share the things that made a positive difference.

First, listen to and rely upon those with experience and training in learning disabilities. We are fortunate to live at a time when learning disabilities are not attributed to laziness or lack of intelligence. Proven therapies, technologies, teaching methods, and classroom modifications are available to your child. Learn as much as you can about the specifics of your child's disabilities, talk with every expert you can, and take advantage of all available resources. In my experience, professionals who devote themselves to this field are passionate about helping your child.

Second, accept the diagnosis. This allows you to seek intervention as soon as possible, and the earlier a child with learning differences is exposed to appropriate teaching methods and interventions, the better. This can only happen if you and your family accept the diagnosis. Acceptance gives children an explanation for why they have difficulty at school and have to work harder than their peers, one that has nothing to do with levels of intelligence. Alongside the extreme difficulties experienced by a child with learning disabilities you will find incredible strengths.

I have friends who chose to ignore their child's learning disabilities. They decided it would be too damaging to their child's self-esteem to learn the truth, be put in special classes, or get tutoring. Without exception, this proved to be a terrible mistake. These children struggled through school without the needed support. They were denied the opportunity for self-awareness and never learned to advocate for themselves. These two attributes, self-awareness and self-advocacy, are critical for your child.

Third, join a community of the parents of children with learning differences. You will have common challenges and questions not shared by parents of other children. Questions I discussed with my friends include the following:

Should I place my child on stimulant medication?

Does the Orton-Gillingham approach to instruction work for dyslexic children?

How do I obtain accommodations for my child in secondary school?

How do I help my child get extra time for college entrance exams?

Other parents who were struggling with the same issues became an invaluable source of not only information but also emotional support.

Finally, remain confident that your family will find its own path and take its own journey. While it might differ from the one you envisioned, it will be equally wonderful and rewarding. You will work alongside fabulous tutors, dedicated teachers, and exceptional experts. You will create strong bonds with families who share your concerns and worries. With your guidance, your children will understand their weaknesses and discover their strengths. They will learn to advocate for themselves and become independent along the way. Your accomplished and talented adult children will be your proof. Best of luck!

—K. R. Maxwell

A NIGHT WITHOUT TEARS

I am delighted and more than a bit relieved that my dyslexic son, AW, has grown into a successful, confident, and respected man. His journey included its share of bumps, detours, and flat tires, for sure.

After two years at the Schenck School, a rigorous language boot camp for dyslexic students, where my son mastered the basics, he entered Woodward Academy's Transition Program. It was the right place and time for him. The Transition Program was large enough that those in it avoided the stigma of being a "sped" (special education student). There were popular kids, athletes, and musicians—same as in any program—so being a part of it carried no shame. It was also very helpful that the stated goal of the Transition Program was to mature out of it—not to stay on a separate track.

Despite the size of the program, teachers paid attention to individual students. At the end of eighth grade, AW's math teacher proposed that she tutor him and one other student so they could begin Algebra 1 in ninth grade rather than a year behind other students. For AW, having a dynamic teacher and a lovely young girl as his fellow student significantly increased the appeal of cramming a year of math into one summer! I think it was also a point of pride that he could master a subject and advance so quickly.

The diversity of students in the Transition Program helped AW find and accept himself, with his talents, his weaknesses, and his learning disability. That self-acceptance became the underpinning of adult self-confidence.

Struggling with reading and writing has made AW an incredibly compassionate person. I think he came to understand that everyone has some difficulty and that being judgmental is not only wrong but also a barrier to understanding. In his career as a manager, AW has focused on helping those who work for him rather than simply criticizing. Middle school can be a time of supreme self-absorption and blindness to the struggles of others, but AW's own struggles made him sympathetic to the challenges others face.

I was tired of being the homework police. I recall laughing, at one point, that a successful evening was one when no one cried.

Still, middle school was hard—for AW and our family. I was tired of being the homework police. I recall laughing, at one point, that a successful evening was one when no one cried. I also learned that sometimes "good enough" was truly good enough; the effort to get to "outstanding" was often not worth the emotional strain. AW's teachers set high standards and expected students to meet them. I learned that it was my role to stand back and be supportive, encouraging, and loving, and to let the teachers be the enforcers. Naturally, when AW complained about teachers being too hard or not fair, I pointed out that this was excellent training for life. Some bosses might be too hard and it was his job to learn how to succeed and please those people.

After AW's numerous trips to the school nurse with headaches and stomach aches in seventh grade, I understood that these ailments were only a proxy for school stress and anxiety. It was not productive for him to have to leave school early or spend hours in the nurse's office. We came to an agreement that he could just call for a mental health day and stay home from school, no questions asked. Miraculously, it seemed, he only used that option once. In hindsight, allowing him to have some control over his life—an exit strategy—worked. He could judge whether or not he was up to the challenge of a school day, and he always was.

I am grateful to Woodward for the multitude of opportunities—in the classroom, on stage, on athletic fields, in service work and clubs. Each student could find a place to shine there. The student body was diverse enough that cliques seemed to be the exception rather than the norm. The teachers were invested in the success of each student and attentive to different ways of learning rather than relying on a single way of teaching and expecting students to adjust.

In some of the dark hours, I reminded AW that formal education would only represent about 20 percent of his life and that, after high school, he would chart his own course. Happily, his course included college (with the selection process less than discreetly parent managed). He is now very successful in his career, happily married, self-confident, and content with himself. Who could ask for more?

—LW

LET YOUR REACH EXCEED YOUR GRASP

What do you do when you are told that your child has a learning difference (disability)? Suddenly the rug is pulled out from under you. This was not in your plan, and you are at a loss as to how to correct the situation. The earth shifts again when you are told that it is not going to be "corrected." Instead, your child must learn to work around this very difficult obstacle to academics, not just for this month or year, but for all the years ahead. This was what my wife and I heard when we were told that our first-grader would need a special school in order to begin his arduous academic journey.

I he testing that brought us to that point was bittersweet. It identified problem areas, but this was somehow comforting because for the first time, we knew where the problems lay. Up to then, all we knew was that school created great anxiety and unhappiness in our son. He felt like a failure and so did we, as loving parents who wanted only the best for our child. He was already in one of the best private schools in the area, but the curriculum was not geared for students with learning differences. He needed a class designed to help him compensate in other ways and not continue to hit his head against that immovable brick wall.

A proper class designed to meet his learning needs, however, was only the beginning of years of struggling as other issues surfaced. We didn't realize then that learning new ways of learning requires enormous mental energy and schoolwork must be interspersed with other activities such as sports, play, and free time. A child has to recharge his energy bank for more academics. Self-esteem issues arose, and even anger, centered on the question, Why me?

While help is available, auxiliary issues will probably arise on the journey you now find yourself taking. Don't be surprised to find that you too will need encourage-ment and emotional support from time to time. Reading this book will confirm that the feelings and frustrations

> *The feelings and frustrations you're experiencing are not unique to you.*

you're experiencing are not unique to you. This is a long

journey, and each year, you will find that the struggle for both you and your child remains.

The good news is that if you stop for a moment and look back to where you were at the beginning of this journey, you will see great progress. We are proud of my son's many accomplishments. It took much determination, energy, time, and work for him to graduate from UGA and find the satisfying career he now enjoys with a terrific company. He has a wonderful wife and family, and best of all, deep empathy for others. He is always polite, courteous, and helpful.

I cannot think of any way I would change my son. What we called a learning difference (disability), and what produced such fear in us at the beginning I now recognize as a tool that God used to bless us all. We all have grown in ways that none of us could have foreseen. Persevere and don't look at the circumstance but, instead, at the vision of where you are heading. As the saying goes, always let your reach exceed your grasp.

—H. Miller

CONTINUOUS PROBLEM SOLVING

Perhaps my husband and I should have suspected that life with the two eldest of our three sons would be different when we discovered that one had only nineteen baby teeth and the other had twenty-one. One consumed books like food; the other refused to read. The one who read constantly couldn't grasp the world of sequencing, was self-sufficient, and not competitive. The other was a whiz with numbers and obsessed with winning.

We thought nothing of our eldest son's mispronouncing words. He was beyond bright and loved learning, and was far more mature than most of his friends. We first became concerned when he grew frustrated with science and math. He was also diagnosed as tone deaf in the second grade, our second clue that something was amiss. His father and I can't sing either, so we didn't think much about it.

We had our first son tested in the fourth grade. He scored off the charts for ability and learning. No surprise there, but the results also revealed learning disabilities, a subject we knew nothing about.

He continued at his private school into the fifth grade, when we transferred him to Woodward Academy, which had a unique program for students with learning disabilities. The ISP program, as it was called, allowed our son to learn in his own way. He always made good grades, but the program allowed him to reach new heights and was something of a miracle to us—and to him.

Our concern for our second son grew when he collapsed on the floor, weeping, after seeing that his younger brother by a year got better grades. No assurance his father and I gave him helped. Following our experience with our eldest, we worried about the struggles our second son might face. We moved him into Woodward's ISP program as a fourth-grader.

The eldest moved on from the ISP program relatively early. He was an honor-roll student and his learning disabilities— audio discrimination and sequencing—were ever-present but well managed. He studied Latin, a godsend that we didn't appreciate until college. He was accepted at three outstanding colleges, with full scholarships at two, and decided to attend Davidson.

His learning disabilities affected him there, when he did miserably in German, and he needed to find a way to work around them. He went back to Latin and continued to succeed in a difficult educational environment. He graduated and later earned an MBA at Wake Forest. Today, he has his own business, something we never imagined, and he has been extremely successful.

When our second son was thirteen, Woodward expressed concerns about his ability to graduate. "Mom, if they'll just let me stay there, I promise I'll graduate," he said. Sounds simple enough; we were increasingly impressed by this child's determination to succeed.

The major drawback, which we had no way of realizing at the time, was that his learning disability was never correctly diagnosed but given the vague label of "word-processing problems."

From ticket sales for a Boy Scouts show to an Eagle Scout project that turned out to be the biggest in the

Atlanta Area Council, he showed great drive and competitive spirit, but his battles in the classroom continued.

He graduated from Woodward and attended Loyola
University in New Orleans but came home after one
semester. According to school policy, a student having
academic trouble has to sit out one semester before
returning. He went back to Loyola and managed until the
end of his junior year, when he faced more difficulties.

I contacted the acting dean of the School of Business
to explain my perspective on ways the college might
not be meeting his needs despite its learning disabilities program. Luckily, the dean was one of the finest
cducators I've met. We agreed that my son would be
tested at a facility approved by the college. The school
would review the test results and *if* it were determined
that he could succeed, he could return without missing
a semester.

The testing took place over ninc hours in one day. The
goal was to discover the basic problem. The diagnosis,
which had eluded us for years, was dyslexia.

My son was relieved to finally label his learning disability, and I was equally relieved to see a path forward for his earning his college degree. Earn it, he did. For the first time in his life, he made As and Bs, and even represented Loyola in a competition to develop outstanding business plans. Tutoring on how to cope with dyslexia put him over the hurdle that had plagued him throughout his education.

Prior to graduation, the president of an Atlanta company hired him to begin work as soon as he finished college. The company went national, and our son now heads its sales division, his natural inclination toward competition flourishing daily.

It's funny to recall that, one day, when someone did something to get me going, and I was expressing my serious displeasure, our middle son piped up and said, "Mom, I don't know what you are so upset about. You have three college graduates, three Eagle Scouts, and no one has been in jail." Out of the mouths of babes. We are beyond blessed.

Much of my sons' success is a tribute to programs like the one at Woodward, where dedicated teachers understand how the minds of special children work and pave the way for them to make their marks on the world. Learning in a different way does not have to hamper learning.

And, by the way, the eldest, who, we were told, couldn't carry a tune, sings beautifully, right on key.

—Margaret O. Blackstock

CHAPTER 9

CELEBRATE THE DIFFERENCE IN THE CLASSROOM

(Voices of Teachers)

H ow do you teach students who have learning disabilities? As one teacher reflects here, there is no magic formula. What works best for most won't work for all, she maintains, pointing out the importance of different strokes for different folks. As the title of this chapter's second essay, "Teaching Children and Subject Matter," implies, the good teacher listens to students as they respond to various requirements. In "The Most Rewarding Part of My Career," Henry acknowledges the importance of a nonthreatening relationship between instructor and student. The academic environment must support students, granting them the freedom to try and to fail as they seek ways to be successful. Barbara reflects on what it would be like for her to sit in her own classroom and shares an interview with Bill, who recounts details of his difficult journey.

Some strategies work for all, including consistency of expectation, daily accountability, and tasks appropriately broken into manageable segments, but discovering what works best for each individual student must be a joint effort of students and teachers. Both must embrace flexibility and be willing to try, fail, and try again to find new ways of living with and embracing the uniqueness of the disability.

THE MOST REWARDING PART OF MY TEACHING CAREER

My first encounter with learning differences happened within my own family. My first-grader had difficulties in school. The regular classroom instruction was more frustrating than helpful. He grew exceedingly agitated, and going to school became a time for tears—for both child and parents. What to do?

Though I was an educator, I wasn't sure. Slowly, I began to learn about learning differences and strategies for dealing with them, firsthand. My understanding of different learning styles and how to teach to them expanded greatly. However, this came six or seven years later, while teaching science at the Woodward Academy Middle School.

I was asked to team-teach a science class with a learning-disabilities specialist. I provided the science expertise and my special-education teammate helped me modify my lessons in ways that would be helpful for our students. I spent the next six years being mentored on strategies for teaching students with learning differences. It was without question the most rewarding part of my teaching career.

I came to understand that we all have learning differences and difficulties to varying degrees—some are simply more troublesome than others. Viewed in this light, what used to be thought of as "disabilities" are really just differences that can be addressed with the right techniques and teaching strategies.

I came to understand that we all have learning differences and difficulties to varying degrees— some are simply more troublesome than others.

When the pathways to successful storage, retrieval, application, and synthesis of information and concepts are interrupted, we must develop new pathways, or modify or strengthen the existing pathways. The teacher should be ready to alter traditional teaching techniques and to proceed always with patience and consistency.

The following are some suggestions regarding learning differences gleaned from my years of working with the special-education mentor at Woodward.

Low self-confidence is a deterrent to learning. Students who have met with academic failure often hesitate to try for fear of failing again. To remedy this mindset, the teacher must create an atmosphere of trust. Baby steps at first lead to bigger steps later. The only reward for complying must be academic success. I have never seen happier faces than those registering new milestones where they once knew only disappointment. In such an atmosphere, the teacher becomes a valuable link to success, and trust deepens. A little self-confidence goes a long way.

Automating skills, routines, and consistency make learning pathways stronger and more automatic. The student's full attention and energy can then be given to the new material at hand. Here are some routines I have found helpful:

1. Always have students use paper and pencil to solve problems (show steps), answer questions, create a paragraph, demonstrate principles, spell and define words, and so on. The tactile process of using paper and pencil helps to develop learning pathways and make learning automatic.

2. Use a storyline to teach new material. Connecting a silly story to a concept allows students to retrieve it by remembering the story.

3. Use acrostics and acronyms for easy retrieval of lists and sequences.

4. Have students create and daily review flash cards that contain vocabulary definitions, concepts, and principles they are currently studying. This helps with the storage, retrieval, and application of material.

5. A slightly different approach is to ask students to keep a daily journal of main ideas discussed

in class by using class notes and worksheets to rethink what they did that day. Formulating the lesson's main ideas requires higher-level processing, so it works best for mastering concepts, not introducing new ideas.

6. Always use the same language on tests that you used when teaching the material. This helps the retrieval process. Tests are for assessment not surprises.

7. Make tests powerful learning experiences. Have students correct all errors after the test is graded. Ask them to write out why they missed a question. Was it a reading error, failure to review that concept the night before, carelessness, or haste? Self-evaluation can be a valuable learning tool.

8. Last but certainly not least, parents must provide a comfortable, quiet, and well-lit desk/work area for the student at home. A consistent daily time for homework, study, and reading is essential.

Students must discover, often by trial and error, the techniques and strategies that work best for them. Yes, it takes work and determination, but that effort can be the beginning of living successfully *with,* and not *in spite of,* a learning difference.

—Henry

TEACHING CHILDREN AND SUBJECT MATTER

Teaching in the Transition Program at Woodward Academy from 1987 to 2001 was one of the great privileges of my life. It was an ideal situation for a teacher because I had small classes—never more than fifteen students—which allowed me to focus on the individual.

I had been teaching for many years when I came to Woodward. I had some experience with LD students, but I also had a lot to learn in order to be the best teacher I could be for them.

For starters, I learned that these middle-school students of above-average intelligence wanted to succeed academically but did not learn in traditional academic ways. Sometimes, because of their mental ability, they developed habits that were not the best for them long-term. For example, if they were auditory learners, they might pick up most of what they needed for tests just by listening well in the classroom. That prevented their developing the study habits they would need long term. This was true even of the most motivated students.

Students in seventh and eighth grade are not fully mature. They don't always advocate for themselves or analyze the changes they need to make in self-discipline. This does not mean that they don't want to succeed, however, and sometimes that truth appears. I remember one student, a savvy athlete, who told me, "Would you please require the tutorial for me? If you do, it could become a habit." He knew himself well enough to realize that he needed that requirement and to ask for it.

I learned that my assignments had to be broken down into smaller tasks if students were to have a chance of success. In my first year of teaching Transition students, I would break the task down into manageable parts, or so I thought. When it failed with most of the students, I had to go back and break it down further.

Over time, I found a system that worked. If the larger task was to analyze a story, for instance, my first assignment might be to look up the vocabulary needed to comprehend it. The second task would be to read the story and list ten plot events in order. The third assignment required them to list and identify the characters. Only when those lower-level tasks had been completed would I put a question on a test requiring higher-level thinking about motive, consequences, or underlying theme.

I learned that words are inadequate to motivate students who have had limited academic success or who know shortcuts that enable them to get by. If the grade doesn't catch them, few make changes. Again, because of their intelligence, my students could pass tests. I had to convince them that the small daily tasks were just as important in creating long-term memory and a disciplined approach to learning.

I began weighting the daily class work the same as the tests and essays for grading, and I gave zeros for work not done. The effect of this strategy was that the weaker students who did the daily work passed even if they did poorly on tests and essays. The stronger students who could manage the tests but neglected daily work did not did not make As and Bs. There is nothing like grades to get a message through to both students and parents.

I always believed that my students were worthy of my best efforts. But I also found out that students with learning differences, especially the ones with attention problems, would roll the dice when deciding whether to do an assignment or not. Once I knew they were thinking that I might not check up on their assignment the next day, I made sure that there was *always* a quiz the day after I assigned a story. There was *always* a check-up on vocabulary the day after I gave the homework, and a rough draft was *always* expected to be turned in as the next composition got started.

When students realized there was a 100 percent chance that assigned work would be graded, the percentage of work done greatly increased. I could do this partly because, as I mentioned earlier, I never had more than fifteen students.

The first year I taught school—many years before I came to teach at Woodward—I settled the issue of whether I would attempt to be popular with the students or give them the knowledge and skills they needed.

I took the second route everywhere I taught. This, of course, meant that some of my Transition students did not always like my style of teaching. That was just fine. My motto, "They'll love me later," has proven true.

Three examples: One young lady wrote me a thank-you note when she graduated from Woodward. "You believed in me before I believed in myself," she wrote. Before I retired, one young man came to the dining hall at Woodward to say, "I wanted you to know that I have graduated from college, and it was possible because of the organizational and study habits I learned in seventh- and eighth-grade English."

Another former student, now a very successful adult, e-mailed me last year: "My sales work is all done by e-mail. My coworkers tease me because I proofread them. They don't understand that I'm just trying to get them to read the way you would like them to be."

Thanks, Woodward and Transition Program for giving me the opportunity to make a difference.

—Jane R. King

BECOMING A STUDENT IN MY OWN CLASSROOM

In my final weeks before retirement, I looked closely at my students and my classroom. The lens changed continually as the days waned and became hours. Students presented their final projects and took their last tests. Their end-of-year efforts completed, they breathed sighs of relief, and those who had sprinted strenuously to cross the finish line expressed pride. Watching and listening, I asked myself the question that intrigued me at the end of every year: would I want to be a student in my classroom?

> *Watching and listening, I asked myself the question that intrigued me at the end of every year: would I want to be a student in my classroom?*

I tried to "read my class" just as I directed my students to "read the classroom" for silent, visual cues on how to proceed. I tried to learn from previous years what worked well, what worked not so well, and what could work better.

Did I grow up wanting to be a teacher? No, but teachers were always my heroes. When I began teaching, my goal was to be a memorable teacher for students. Maybe I could scratch the surface of their learning. Maybe I could awaken a writing genie. Maybe I could push hard enough to stretch their limits. Maybe I could just take the time to listen. Maybe face-to-face, eye-to-eye we could communicate about a special challenge.

Teaching students with learning disabilities challenged every fiber of my teaching soul. I was driven by a passion to learn more so that I could teach from the heart. Entering the world of the learning disabled landed me squarely at the desks of my students. I was in a tech-led environment, teaching students who lived by their laptops, though I didn't know much technology at the time. All students in the Transition Program were supplied with laptops, which they used at home and at school.

My empathy for my students was boundless, partly because I had to learn as much as they did. Like them, I struggled to grasp new concepts, process information, recognize salient details, implement new applications, and persist in the quest to solve problems. Fortunately, many of my students were tech-literate and stepped up to assist when I needed help. This teach-the-teacher role reversal empowered them. I encouraged my students to ask for help along the way as we encountered new lessons, and I wasn't afraid to ask for theirs.

My open invitation to seek help included their coming in for lunch whenever students felt the need. I, in turn, attended as many technology workshops as I could. Such direct instruction equipped me with new multisensory instructional ideas to share with my classes. Smartboard, PowerPoint, and Google applications, as well as various interactive programs, entered my repertoire.

I became a shameless borrower of ideas, weaving *Habits of Mind* by Arthur L. Costa and Bena Kallick into the fabric of my lessons. From the authors' list of sixteen skills, I extrapolated and emphasized the following: Strive for accuracy, take responsible risks, and be aware of and manage impulsivity. As a cook does, I took basic lesson recipes and redesigned them to suit my students. I adapted my classroom yearly, monthly, weekly, daily, even hourly to the barometer of my students. What did not work in my 9 a.m. class I quickly changed for the class at ten.

A few borrowed ideas became staples. From Corbett Harrison, an online teacher of writing, I learned to devote the first ten minutes of class every day to a writing notebook, where students glued ten inviting topics to respond to in the order of their choice. A favorite was "If your pencil could talk, what would it say about you?" Topics were illustrated either with stick figures or clip art. Students chose their own submission time frames before a final deadline, which gave them ownership of their writing and tailored the pace of work to the individual. The flexible schedule also gave them time to look over their writing with a critical eye. Over the years, my mantra became, "Always submit your best. Ask yourself, 'Is this my *best*?' and do not be afraid to do it over."

Online, I discovered interactive notebooks and lap books. We created interactive grammar notebooks, with colorful cut-and-paste flip charts to learn grammar rules, each student compiling his or her own grammar bible. Such fine motor tasks were challenging for some students, and I circulated to assist them, helping each to proceed as best he or she could. The old adage of different strokes for different folks animated numerous lessons.

To encourage the awareness of overused words in writing, we celebrated a funeral for dead words. Each student was assigned a hackneyed word (*get, like, awesome, mad, cool*) for which he or she wrote a eulogy stating how the word had outlived its time and would be replaced with strong synonyms. Tape-recorded funeral music played as the students, led by our principal in his black graduation robe, marched outside to a hole dug in the garden to bury the slip of paper on which their dead word was written. A reception with treats was held at the end of the ceremony. Cognizant of the words in our mass grave, students began self-correcting and even correcting their classmates when any of the departed words crept into writing or conversations.

Poetry became a favorite opportunity for students to build memory skills and to develop self-confidence in public speaking. Selections changed yearly to suit the person-alities of the group. One year, Robert Frost and Maya

Angelou stood out. Students chose poems by these poets, and in addition to memorizing Frost's "Stopping by Woods on a Snowy Evening" and Angelou's "Life Doesn't Frighten Me," students donned costumes and interpreted the poems.

We memorized Dr. Martin Luther King Jr.'s "I Have a Dream" speech and presented it to the entire school over the videoed morning announcements. We wrote original poems, self-published in a final poetry collection titled, *I'm as Tall as My Eyes,* a name submitted by one of the children. We sent poems to a writing contest, which published several of them. "I've never done this before; I can't write a poem," one of the published students had claimed, backing away from the assignment. A simple prompt—write about what you know—got him back on track and encouraged a marvelous poem about his collections of toys.

Essay writing was nobody's favorite, but that didn't stop us. The Jewish Anti-Defamation League sponsors yearly writing contests focused on the theme of No Place for Hate. In 2016, four of our "learning disabled" students placed for the southern region and were honored at

Kennesaw State University. The admonition to write what you know resulted in essays about a beloved babysitter, an immigrant mother, a doctor/missionary father, and one student's personal hero, Nelson Mandela.

I wish I could say I followed a formula for what worked well some years and flopped others. In some measure, I have always been led and taught by the children. As I yielded to twenty-first-century technology demands, I discovered hidden reserves of personal intellectual rigor. Fear of new material faded as I took a deep breath and dived in. Identifying and attacking my personal disability connected me to my students' varied learning challenges.

Recently I read this quotation by the theologian Howard Thurman: "Over the heads of her students she holds a crown that she challenges them to grow tall enough to wear." Those words summed up my goal for students. My means were never crystal clear at the outset but always emerged as I strived to help my students reach for their personal crowns, place them on their heads, and walk away with pride.

With those words in mind, I believe I can answer in the affirmative the question that consumed my final days of teaching: yes, I would like to have been a student in my class. In fact, I always was.

—Barbara B. Dunbar

REFLECTIONS ON A CHILD

As a student in my sixth-grade class at Woodward Academy, Bill struggled socially and academically. He was a good kid with great potential, but test results and early school performance indicated that he was also at risk in many areas.

After not seeing them for eight years, I met him and his mom at a Starbucks as Bill was departing to the Midwest for his first job. He had just graduated cum laude from University of South Carolina (USC) and was going to work for a big insurance company. Clearly, he'd found a way to manage the areas where he once seemed to be at risk, and I was curious to hear how he and his mother saw the path that ultimately led to his success.

"Such an achievement," Mom said of Bill's performance at USC, "when his formal testing suggested a questionable degree of success for him in the middle school and then upper school at Woodward Academy."

"So, how did you do it?" I asked Bill.

He could not point to many signs of success in his years at Woodward. He recalled being combative in the elementary school, where he had trouble making and keeping friends. He said that he simply was not academically motivated in those years.

I asked what he had found hard about his time in sixth grade, when I had him in class. He remembered struggling to recite poetry and the Gettysburg Address. Composing poems, journal writing, and spelling were tough too. There were fights with a male classmate and various arguments. On the plus side, he recalled, with a smile, a project created with a partner for the annual market day and another on the Civil War for a social studies class. He joined the scrabble club I sponsored and excelled there, as well as in the chess club.

Mom recalled numerous challenges requiring numerous interventions in those early years. I taught at a school Bill had attended prior to Woodward, one for students with learning disabilities. I did not have Bill in my class then but knew of the emotional outbursts that punctuated his years there. He pushed the limits with his fits of anger and stubborn refusals to comply with teachers' requests.

At an interview for admission to another school, he crossed his arms, planted himself firmly in a chair, and refused to answer a single question. The interview at Woodward fared better, thanks to a sympathetic interviewer and a chair that Bill found quite comfortable.

The summer of his rising seventh-grade year, I took him for frozen yogurt. I wanted him to know that I would miss hIm and that I believed he could master himself, behaviorally and academically. After moving on at Woodward, Bill occasionally crossed the campus to say hello. Never one much for words, he would just check in, smile, give a hug, and be on his way.

He had plenty of help identifying and managing the various risks he faced in his academic career. "When your child is hurting, you do everything you can to help," Mom said.

Aside from parental support and academic help at Woodward, Bill attended therapy sessions, went to social sensitivity groups, and participated in summer camps. He did not claim that any one strategy turned him around. "I was just not motivated," he said.

Mom agreed. "Not even money inspired you," she said.

Were there any positives in the upper school? Bill felt that getting extra tutoring to prepare for tests and writing papers at Woodward served him well in college. It was only during his second round of prepping for the ACT test that he realized he would have to take it seriously or he would be "on his own for college."

At University of South Carolina, he toyed with the idea of becoming a banker or accountant, but those fields didn't hold his interest. Eventually, he settled on a career path to be a risk management specialist with an insurance company and a first job that would take him to the Midwest two days after we met at Starbucks.

The kid who'd scored low in critical thinking skills years ago was now explaining that he was excited about the challenge of assessing high versus acceptable risk in various corporate scenarios. This was the little boy whose mother, on the brink of tears, used to wait outside my classroom to find out how his day had gone.

My query about his gains in maturity brought huge nods and smiles from both his mother and Bill. He agreed that he grew to accept academic challenges, gained confidence in himself socially, and became appreciative of his parents' support. Much more vocal and confident than the boy I remembered, he smiled, gave me hug, and promised to stay in touch as he went on his way.

—Bill, as told to B. Brown

CHAPTER 10
CREATIVE ALTERNATIVES

"**M**y learning disability does not disable me." The motto of one contributor to this chapter expresses a desire shared by all of them: not to be defined or limited by a learning difference.

How do different learners avoid labels and limitations when conventional instruction and learning strategies don't work? The first step is recognizing and accepting what is effective for long-term learning and what isn't. Each learner must try a smorgasbord of ideas, discard those that don't work and embrace those that do, though this is not always the fastest route.

In all of these accounts, the key steps to finding the right strategies are recognition, creative thinking, and the use of resources including special note-taking methods, assistive technology, family support, and using strengths to compensate for nonstrengths. Some readers will see familiar methods here, and hopefully, others will find the inspiration to develop and hone the strategies that work best for them.

THE ADD ADVANTAGE

Many see attention-deficit disorder as a major impediment in life and focus on the potential negatives. Growing up, I was a fanatic about the positives. ADD forced me to find creative ways to overcome life's obstacles, to be adaptive to situations, and to work hard. While it did present certain difficulties, it also provided experiences that would become invaluable later, in my career.

> *ADD forced me to find creative ways to overcome life's obstacles, to be adaptive to situations, and to work hard.*

In high school, I knew I had to set myself apart in applying for college because my grades were not going to do it, and nor would loading my application with volunteer work for charities or other organizations. I needed something original to mark my application, something that I enjoyed and was passionate about, something that would clearly differentiate me from my classmates.

I decided I would start a FIRST (For Inspiration and Recognition of Science and Technology) Robotics team at my high school. The FIRST robotics program encourages entrepreneurship in science and technology. High school teams from around the country are given six weeks to design, engineer, and build a working robot that can perform a series of tasks while meeting a strict set of specifications. Practicing engineers serve as mentors to the students, who gain real-world experience in mechanical design, programming, and corporate fundraising.

I thought this would be an easy sell to my school's headmaster. I was wrong. I could not gain the necessary administrative support, and interested staff had other commitments. In trying to start a team, though, I made contacts who helped me join an existing team based at the Georgia Institute of Technology. Things didn't work out exactly as I'd planned, but my efforts and subsequent work on the Georgia Tech team gave me a leg up on college applications and showed a degree of responsibility and leadership that set me apart.

ADD has forced me to maneuver around obstacles to achieve. In high school, that meant getting accepted to Clemson, and at Clemson, it meant graduating with an engineering degree. I learned to set a goal, determine how to get there, and then figure out, one step at a time, how to manage any negatives.

Looking back on college and my career, ADD was a hindrance at times, but learning how to overcome its challenges contributed hugely to my success. I can now problem-solve and engineer solutions better than many of my coworkers, thanks in part to the creative work-arounds my ADD demanded.

—David

MY DISABILITY DOES NOT DEFINE ME

My motto has always been: My learning disability does not disable me!

I am extremely organized. I could have made all As in school, but I was distracted. I focused on a variety of abilities—athletics, art, social skills—and never saw my wide range of nonacademic interests as the symptom of a disability. School simply did not have my attention.

Woodward saved me. The Transition Program was amazing. Its motto at the time, "Every opportunity for every student," was delivered every single day. I wasn't going to be in an AP class or on the debate team, but I did make the varsity soccer team as a ninety-pound freshman. I had confidence, and I owe that to my teachers and coaches.

That confidence stayed with me at the University of Mississippi. There were plenty of distractions at Ole Miss. I wasn't there on a scholarship, but I ended my college career on the chancellor's honor roll, and I did that all on my own. I could learn and pay attention; it just took a little extra work.

After college, I soared in the corporate world. I was different and had "creative ideas." But my disabilities came back in other ways—for instance, when I realized how hard it can be to complete a task, or to decide where to start one. Scary stuff! I came face-to-face with daily struggles that my parents and teachers saw all along. Medicine was never an option for me. I didn't like or want it. I can do this on my own, I thought, and I did.

Now, I work for a nonprofit organization as the director of operations, while raising my two beautiful daughters with my husband.

Having ADHD has never been an excuse for me, and I owe that to my teachers and parents, who taught me the skills to live, learn, and achieve with my learning obstacles. Nothing gives me more pride than seeing the achievements of Woodward Academy's Transition students. We all have a story, and we are gifted in so many ways.

—Meg

NOTE CARDS FOR EVERYTHING

I was not the type of student who could just sit down, read a book, and learn the information. I learned differently, and after I was diagnosed, I knew I had to find another way. It was my mother who came up with the idea of using note cards to help me absorb what I needed to learn. I would read something and then write out multiple-choice or fill-in-the-blank questions about it on note cards. My mom used the note cards to quiz me.

What a difference this strategy made! Note cards helped me retain names in history, learn definitions for English, and facts for science. I could absorb information, it turned out, but I had to have it drilled into me, or it wouldn't stick. The note-card quiz method allowed me to learn the material I needed for all of my classes.

My parents worked hard at helping me find ways to succeed. I was always willing to put in the time, but I needed that guidance to really improve. My teachers were a big help too. I'm not sure where I would be without my parents and teachers; they were such a big part of my success.

—Charles

A COLOR-CODED LIFE

I always had trouble getting organized, and organization is one of the keys to success. Several tools proved invaluable. I could not have gotten through school without flash cards. I put them in rings to keep them organized and color-coded them by subject. Whatever the class, I studied for it using those color-coded flash cards, and today, long after finishing school, I have adapted the same system to organize daily life. I color-code my paper calendar, for instance, just as I once did those flash cards, with each of my children's activities highlighted by name and a distinct color.

Time management offered another breakthrough. I realized at some point that I needed to plan well in advance in order to be successful. The night before just wasn't going to cut it. A full week before I had a test, I would gather all my notes and study materials and organize them to start studying. Years later, coordinating the demands of family and work, I still try to plan my time efficiently and begin working on important tasks well in advance. Tools like these aren't complicated, but they proved invaluable in helping me to learn how I learn best and to succeed in school and in life.

—**Mary**

THINKING OUTSIDE THE BOX

The beginning of my education was rough. When teachers discovered that I was not progressing as expected in kindergarten, my parents had me tested for learning difficulties. I was diagnosed and enrolled in a special school. To make a bad situation worse, I had to repeat first grade. After four years of intense remediation, I was allowed to transfer to Woodward Academy, a college preparatory school with a special program for different learners. My academic career there was not stellar, but I graduated and entered UGA, where I graduated with a degree in finance from the Terry School of Business. Getting the degree wasn't easy. Different tools work for different people, but here are some of the challenges, strategies for surviving, and strengths I encountered over the years:

Challenges

□ Setbacks often seem worse than they are. In ninth-grade biology class, everyone had to care for a living creature. I thought a bird would be easy, but his beak fell off, and he died. I was sure I would fail the class for that, but I didn't.

□ I have difficulty initiating work. Organizing projects and tasks is tough.

□ I am not good with details. At one point, I paid my bills by averaging them and sending each vendor the average amount (luckily, my wife now handles the household bills).

▫ I need to be given a road map to figure a course of action.

Strategies

▫ Do what your buddy does. In kindergarten, I was so intent on copying a friend's paper, I even copied his name. Watching your buddy to keep up with class procedures is a good idea, but it can go too far.

▫ Learn to manage the system. I played in a band in high school and wanted long hair for performances, but the school had a strict haircut code. I bought a wig that met the school's standard and wore it to classes every day. I never got detentions for *my* long hair because no one ever saw it.

▫ Ask a teacher or supervisor to set a firm deadline for tasks. Nothing motivates like a concrete due date.

▫ Take one course less than a full load. I did this every semester during college, and it made things infinitely more manageable.

▫ Take the hundred-year view: what difference will X or Y make in 100 years? The road is long; growth is inconsistent and unpredictable. What seems like a big deal now might not be in the long term.

▫ Practice being intentional. You can't rely on incidental learning.

Strengths

▫ I recognize learning differences in others and treat them with understanding and compassion.

▫ I accept learning differences as a way of life and do not feel negative stigma regarding them.

▫ I and other friends with learning disabilities have "the millionaire mind": IQs that are average to above-average coupled with the capacity to be successful in areas of strength.

▫ I can use strengths to manage nonstrengths.

—Wilson

Spreading Hope One
Story at a Time

No two people achieve success in the same way. Much like the ways our contributors needed to be creative with their learning styles, they also needed to be creative with how they became successful—academically, personally, and professionally. Despite their setbacks, they found the determination and perseverance to achieve what they once thought impossible. The voices of our contributors speak volumes for the countless amount of people living with learning differences. While their stories are unique, their struggles are not. Specialized and appropriate education and support from schools, teachers, and parents alike is the first step in building a lasting foundation for students' educational success and confidence.

Schools that specialize in helping students with learning differences are invaluable tools for families everywhere. They validate the myriad of learning difficulties their students struggle with as well as provide a feeling of acceptance and inclusion for all students regardless of their learning style. No students should be discouraged from learning simply because they do it differently. Of course, schools are only as strong as their teachers. By instilling confidence and pride into the work of their students, teachers can completely change students' attitudes and performance in school. Each success story in this book was possible, in part, because of dedicated and hardworking teachers and schools. Let these stories be a source of inspiration for those teaching students with learning differences of all kinds. Teachers and parents can work hand-in-hand in creating a conducive learning environment. All children look to their parents for love, support, and guidance. Parents must set the example for what they wish to see their children achieve. If a child is expected to never give up and persevere through the rough patches, that behavior has to begin with the parents. As the parents who told their stories assert, having a child with learning differences isn't easy. A strong belief in one's own abilities coupled with persistence and patience can make the difference between failure and success—for parents and children alike.

While teachers and parents are integral to the stories in this book, they do not represent the book's purpose, which is to celebrate the triumphs of those who were written off as less-than, stupid, lazy, or simply unable to learn. For those with learning differences, perhaps the greatest resource is the stories of others. Stories such as "The Hunter Instinct" are inspirational to those who may have to fight against a lack of resources and need an extra push of determination to achieve success. "Burning Pants" teaches us that discovering unique passions that may differ from daily academics allows children to develop a sense of purpose and self-confidence. Participating in outside activities may also reinforce the feeling of normalcy these children may lack in academic settings. "How ADD Helped SEAL the Deal" exemplifies how accepting one's learning difference can be used to advantage. Through self-discovery and perseverance, Sam B was able to overcome the adversity of his ADD and succeed in one of the military's hardest training programs. Self-knowledge and self-acceptance are gateways to new accomplishments. In fact, throughout this book our contributors have repeatedly referenced the importance of self-knowledge.

None of us can truly be confident in our abilities without knowing and accepting who we are. Embracing our unique strengths and learning to manage our ever-present nonstrengths is another strategy that makes a distinct difference between success and failure. Taking advantage of available resources to manage nonstrengths is an act of courage and strength and not a sign of a deficit or weakness. Above all, we should remember that having a learning difference may mean hidden talents, nestled just below the surface, that can be discovered and lead to self-fulfillment and a self-actualized life. If you or your child has a learning difference, take the advice of those who have spoken through this book and don't be afraid of creative learning.

REFERENCES

ATLANTA SPEECH SCHOOL

The Atlanta Speech School inspires transformative changes in the lives of children and adults through research-based practices, innovation, advocacy, and partnerships with other organizations. Because of the Atlanta Speech School, each child in attendance, and every child in Georgia, can acquire the language and literacy abilities essential for deciding his or her own future.

SCHENCK SCHOOL

The Schenck School's mission is to build a solid educational foundation for students with dyslexia and to develop their rich potential. The Schenck School is widely regarded as one of the top schools for dyslexic students in the United States.

WOODWARD ACADEMY

Woodward Academy offers unparalleled opportunities in academics, the arts, and athletics—including the Transition

Learning Support Program. Woodward's Transition program, one of the first in Atlanta to educate students with diagnosed learning differences in a college preparatory setting, continues to educate bright students who learn differently in an inclusive environment dedicated to developing critical thinkers and ethical problem solvers.

MAKING A DIFFERENCE

Profits from the sale of this book and all revenue from contributions will go to the Creative Learners Project of the Dyslexia Resource for the purpose of training site coordinators in Communities in Schools to recognize and address learning differences. Communities In Schools (CIS) was founded by Bill Milliken to bring community resources inside public schools where they are personal, coordinated, and accountable. Now Serving 1.57 million students and their families in more than 2,300 schools in 25 states and the District of Columbia, CIS builds relationships that empower students to stay in school and succeed in life.

The Dyslexia Resource, a partner with Communities in Schools, is an Atlanta-based nonprofit organization created and working in partnership with The Schenck School. The mission of the DR is to facilitate teacher training, champion the support of students and parents, and educate the public about dyslexia. For more information contact the Dyslexia Resource, visit www. dyslexiaresource.org/contact/.

ABOUT THE AUTHOR

Selma Ridgway has spent the majority of her career in the field of education. Most notably, she spent 26 years at Woodward Academy where she directed the Transition Program, a program designed to meet the needs of creative learners. Prior to working with the special population of creative learners, Selma taught high school mathematics, coached interscholastic policy debate, and worked as a school counselor. During those years she practiced intense critical listening and learned to recognize the different patterns of thinking and learning in her students. Selma then became passionate about partnering with students whose learning styles are different or unconventional and left the school setting in 2008 to form her own business, Ridgway Coaching. Selma's business allows her to be a fulltime life coach to individuals of all ages who march to the beat of a different drummer. Using compassionate listening, Selma says she learned most of what she knows about different learning styles from the individuals with whom she has worked. She continues to partner with students and adults in helping them make sense of a world that does not always recognize and understand creative learners. Visit www.ridgwaycoaching.com to connect with and contact Selma.